FORGED
BY
LIMITATIONS

WHAT PEOPLE ARE SAYING

"Mr. Last's grueling, but ultimately uplifting personal story should serve as an inspiration not only for people with CP or other disabilities but for anyone who is grappling with obstacles in life."
—Josh Blue comedian

"I commend David for sharing his deeply personal story. To open up to the world about one's physical challenges and unique life journey, especially when that includes dark days that at times seem uncertain and potentially hopeless is incredibly brave. Expressing one's vulnerability is extremely difficult, yet so important as readers will no doubt place their own vulnerabilities and challenges in perspective when reading David's story. And the strength and triumph exhibited by David can only help propel all who read his thought provoking, touching and inspiring story to live life to the fullest with a fresh and a healthier perspective."
—Dr. Noah Makovsky, pediatrician

WHAT PEOPLE ARE SAYING

"As his principal, I greeted David at the front door nearly every school day for four (three?) years of middle school. Despite his daily struggle just to walk through the doors, David made most of those days just a little brighter for others, inspiring all with his positivity and strength. He burdened none of us with the weight he bore. But exhaustion, resentment and anger grew within. Born with cerebral palsy, David battled significant physical limitations, endless rounds of surgery and a sense of differentness. Ultimately, the dark realities of his life nearly cost him his own. In this raw and inspiring memoir, David shares his journey of struggle, resilience, self-discovery, and the people who believed in him along the way. With honesty and courage, he reveals how he found renewed strength in his struggles and purpose in his pain. His story is proof that even in life's hardest moments, hope and triumph are possible."

—Bryan Hay, Middle and High School Principal

FORGED BY LIMITATIONS

DAVID LAST

Storytellers Publishing
Colorado, U.S.A.

Storytellers Publishing
An imprint of Journey Institute Press,
a division of 50 in 52 Journey, Inc.
journeyinstitutepress.org

Copyright © 2025 David Last
All rights reserved.
(All photographs copyrighted to the author
except as noted for public domain images)

Journey Institute Press supports copyright. Copyright allows artistic creativity, encourages diverse voices, and promotes free speech. Thank you for purchasing an authorized edition of this work and for complying with copyright laws by not reproducing, scanning, or distributing any part of this work in any form without permission.

Library of Congress Control Number: Available upon request
Names: Last, David
Title: Forged By Limitations
Description: Colorado: Storytellers Publishing, 2025

Identifiers: ISBN 978-1-964754-40-6 (hardcover)
ISBN 978-1-964754-41-3 (paperback)
ISBN 978-1-964754-42-0 (ebook/kindle)

Subjects: BISAC:
BIOGRAPHY & AUTOBIOGRAPHY / Disability |
BIOGRAPHY & AUTOBIOGRAPHY / Jewish |
SELF-HELP / Motivational & Inspirational |

First Edition
Printed in the United States of America

1 3 5 7 16 39 40 47 50 815

This book was typeset in Baskerville URW / Bebas Neue

Editing by Jessica Medberry, InkWhale Editorial LLC.
Cover design by WiggleB Studios

For my family. Mom, Dad, Grandma, and my siblings, Daniella, Tammy, Avi, Lexie, and my extended family. For constantly pushing me to be the best I could be and seeing my full potential even when I could not see it myself.

To my friends, doctors, and therapists. For accepting me for me and never seeing me as my disability. For always being there when I needed a hand and for teaching me that strength comes in many different forms—for always being in my corner, no matter what.

I could only do this with your help. From the bottom of my heart, thank you all.

For anyone who wants to quit. I have been where you are. Keep up the fight and never give up. This one is for you.

CONTENTS

INTRODUCTION	xi
THE FINAL ROUND	15
WORTH FIGHTING FOR	22
MOMENTS	31
THE CONTENDERS	39
INNER STRENGTH	43
ACCEPTING YOU FOR YOU	49
STEPPING INTO THE RING	58
IT ALL HAPPENS FOR A REASON	63
JUST BE HAPPY	68
THERE IS ALWAYS GOOD	73
THE FIRST ROUND	79
HOPE	83
OKAY TO FAIL	91
NOT BROKEN	97
DOWN ON THE MAT	103
NEVER GIVE UP	108
YOU CAN ALWAYS CHANGE	117
PAIN IN A NEW LIGHT	124
INSPIRATION	132
THE CHAMPION IS NAMED	137
BECAUSE YOU WERE HERE	142
ACKNOWLEDGEMENTS	145
ABOUT THE AUTHOR	147

INTRODUCTION

It is the author's job to present the reader with a point of view different from their own and let the reader decide what they want to do with it. This must be a give-and-take relationship. I give you my story and everything that comes with it, and you internalize what you have heard and use it in any manner you see fit. With such a tall task before me, you have the right to know who I am. What has happened in my life that gives me license to tell you my story.

After all, you have no idea who the hell I am, and I have no idea who you are. We could cross on the street and neither of us would be the wiser. So, what gives me the right to tell you anything? Look, I promise I will not pretend to know who you are. I only want to tell you my story and everything I have gained. I have no right to tell you how to live, and I give you my word that I will never try to. I will make suggestions, but that is where I will stop. All I want to do is tell you the story of my life. Believe me when I say, I am getting more out of telling my story than you are by hearing it. All I ask is that you please hear me out and decide what you want to do with what you have heard. That being said, who exactly am I?

When I was twelve months old, I was diagnosed with cerebral palsy (CP for short). CP is a neurological condition that causes my brain to continuously send messages to my muscles to make them tighten up. These signals cause trouble with my balance and weakness in my muscles, to put it very simply. Because of this, it is challenging for me to move around, affecting all facets of my daily life, from the physical aspects to my cognitive skills.

On my journey through life, I have faced many obstacles. I have had a total of eight surgeries so far, some planned and some not. I've had many types of therapy—physical, occupational, and psychological, in one form or another—since the age of three. I have had battles with depression and other emotional problems, and more falls than I care to count, just to name a few. Also, I have many learning challenges, such as reading and writing disabilities, so my education came with its own obstacles.

Through hard work, I did my best to look for the bright side of every challenge I faced. I tried my hardest to learn and grow from every experience. With every obstacle, I learned and appreciated a new truth about life. Each challenge allowed me to test my mettle and see what I was truly made of. Through it all, I always tried to prove that my CP would never stop me from doing anything in this life. Unfortunately, this caused me to look at my disability as the villain for many years. It would take me a long time to start seeing my CP in a different light, but more on that later.

More times than I would like to admit, a roadblock would stop me and knock me back on my heels. Yet, the more I failed, the more I comprehended that there were things to be learned in defeat as well. Through my many battles, I came to understand that I could learn just as much from losing as I did from winning. After many years, I realized it was only in defeat that I really saw who I was. In my darkest hours, I learned what being strong truly meant. I could only find out what I was capable of when I had hit rock bottom, and my back was against the wall. In those times, I only had two options: continue to fight for my life or give up.

Through my life experiences, I came to understand something fundamental: Whether I won or lost, I always needed to find a way to keep moving forward and keep pushing myself to be better than I was the day before. It is never about winning or losing. All that matters is growing from each experience and using that newfound knowledge to better myself and the world around me. At a very young age, I understood that life would not be fair, but it was only in my later years that I finally gained some perspective. I had to accept how my life would be, but that did not mean I could not improve it.

All that being said, why did I feel the need to put my life experiences in a book? At the end of the day, it is up to you if you want to listen to me or not. I wanted to write this book because if just one person out there finds what I have to say worthwhile and finds inspiration from my story, then it is all worth it. I think all I really want to do is help somebody, anybody who might be going through hard times. I want to be a voice of hope to someone who feels like giving up. If I can do that, then mission accomplished. So, without further ado, I give you the end of my life.

1 THE FINAL ROUND

As I held the knife firmly in my hand, a few thoughts came to mind. The first was a sense of relief. I knew the pain would stop within a few seconds, and I could rest. I was so tired and felt the world's weight on my shoulders. I was just done with it all. I was drained, numb to everything, and ready for the end. It felt like I no longer had the strength to cry, and my tears were all but dried up. I was beyond the point of any other feeling but anger. Anger at myself, bitterness at my situation, and hatred for every event that made it necessary for me to pick up the instrument of my salvation.

Holding my life choices in my hand, another thought struck me. With just a quick movement, I would turn out the lights forever. However, with that thought did not come fear; instead, it was accompanied by a sense of longing. I was not afraid in the slightest. It was almost as if, subconsciously, I had always known this was how it would end, and now, finally, I consciously knew it, too. No other ending had ever seemed in the cards. With the finality of that thought, I was calmer than I had been in a long time. Looking down at the knife, I knew I was ready.

How the hell did I end up here? I mean, here I am in a room alone, despising myself, tears streaming down my face, ready to end my life and welcome the darkness as my own. I must have screwed up royally somewhere along the way. I did not end up here because I made the right decisions, that's for damn sure, and that felt like the worst of it. Knowing I could blame no one but myself I was responsible for my predicament; there would be no shifting blame on this one. There would be no dodging the truth either. I was the one person who put me here; I had to live with that fact and die by it. I was ready to accept my faults and was prepared to take the punishment I thought was necessary. With my final hour upon me, I wanted only one thing. To use my last bit of strength to finish the job and find the peace I so desperately wanted.

Really, I mean, how did I end up here? Well, it was one hell of a roller coaster. After everything I had been through, every battle I had fought, it felt a little stupid that being in college was going to be the straw that broke the camel's back. Perhaps it was a culmination of everything in my past that finally got to me. I did not know, and honestly, I did not care.

Graduating from high school was a big deal. I felt like making it to that day somehow validated every obstacle I had faced. High school had been four years of uphill battles. Never having a chance to rest and catch my breath, I faced one challenge after another. It's not that I don't have happy memories of it. High school was a time of growth and joy, but it was also a time filled with trials and pain. Yet, despite the many obstacles, I worked my ass off, both physically and in my academics, and finally I made it to graduation. I could finally end this chapter of my life and start writing a new one.

I chose where I was going for college, and it was in New York that I laid out the next steps for my future. I could not have been more excited; this would be my first real taste of independence. I figured that after all the challenges I had faced, going to college was my grand prize. The funny thing is that the more I went after my future, the more I ignored the warning signs. I had sacrificed a lot because of my condition. I was forced to grow up way too fast and resented my CP for it. It often felt like I had to choose between being a teenager or treating my disability. I always put my condition first because I knew I needed to, but it meant that I lost out on much of my life during high school. I hated that I had to surrender parts of my life like this, yet, at the same time, I knew it was all for the greater good. But as I prepared for college, all that was in the past. It was finally going to be my time to shine.

I was possessed with the idea of independence. It was such a foreign concept, and I saw it was mine for the taking in New York. I decided where I wanted to move to and chose what school to attend. It seemed like, for the first time in my life, I had complete control over my life. I had a big chip on my shoulder when I left home. I wanted to prove to everyone, and most importantly myself, that my condition would not always run my life. For once, I was going to dictate my journey. Despite my disability, I was going to succeed. I was not going to let anything get in my way. I wanted to make this the best time of my life. Because I was so determined to reach my goal, I was blinded and started making one wrong choice after another.

First, I chose to go to a school in Washington Heights. The city would be challenging with my physical limitations, but I thought I was more than ready for that challenge. Maybe I was a little naïve; I do not know. I figured I would deal with each obstacle when I came upon it; I mean, that is what I had done my entire life. I was always like a bull in a china shop when it came to any challenge. I would run through it and whatever scrapes and bruises I got along the way, well the ends justified the means. Maybe I decided on such a physically demanding place because I just wanted to prove how little my CP was going to affect me. Who can say, but I guess hindsight is everything, right?

If my judgment on the difficulty of traversing the city had been my only mistake, things might have turned out differently, but that was not the case. Next up on the road of bad decisions, I decided to live in a single-person dorm room. I chose this for two main reasons. One, it had a bathroom and shower right in the room, making many aspects of self-care that much easier. The second reason was that I thought it would force me to be more sociable. If I knew the alternative would be sitting in a room alone, I would force myself to be more social and find new connections and friends much faster. I am a timid person by nature, and it takes me a while to open up to others. Living in a single dorm room would force me to speed up that process, or so I thought.

On the first account, I was right, but on the second, I was very wrong. Yes, having a bathroom and shower inside the room made many things more manageable. However, I did not force myself to be sociable like I thought I would.

My days consisted of attending classes, hardly talking to people, returning to my room, and feeling isolated. Quickly, the days started to blur together. Soon, I was in a rut that I could not break away from, leading to a deep depression. I felt no genuine enthusiasm for my classes, and I was physically exhausted from having to navigate the city every day, as well as from my constant anxiety. Life was looking pretty grim. My problems bled into one another. I was not sleeping, so I was too tired even to eat, and because I was not eating, I had no energy to move around the city and participate in my classes and doing the schoolwork was next to impossible. Without strength, I would hide in my dorm room by the end of the day, which only heightened my feelings of isolation.

The horrible cycle would repeat itself every day until I felt utterly hopeless and devoid of any emotion except anger. However, because I was so determined to be in control of my life, my biggest mistake was ignoring all these signs of a deepening and worsening darkness. Typically, I would have seen all these red flags for what they were, but in my search for freedom, the worst thing I did was ignore the plethora of warning signs before my eyes.

The more you want something, the more you tend to ignore the warnings. I was so obsessed with being freed from the shackles of my CP that I was blinded to everything going wrong around me. This led to my ultimate downfall. The worst feeling was that I could blame nobody else except myself. No one had forced me to go to New York, no one had forced me to live in a single-person dorm, no one had made all these mistakes except me, and that was the crux of it all. My first chance to prove I could stand on my own two feet despite my disability, and I had just gotten my ass handed to me. I had tried, and I had failed. I had failed myself, and I had failed everyone who believed in me. There was no way around it, no way to spin it or sugarcoat it; I had lost, and there was no coming back from it. I had tried so damn hard to live independently, and all I had proven was that the freedom I wanted so badly would be my downfall. All of this was my fault, and the only thing I could do about it—the last thing—was accept my failures. There was only one thing left I could control.

I looked around this single dorm room that had become my jail cell. I saw the short hallway leading to the bathroom that I had gambled so much on. I saw the mini fridge I kept in the corner, the desk with all my unfinished schoolwork, the barely used bed, and me sitting on the floor in the middle. I saw my dinner, not even half eaten, on the floor next to me. I saw the posters I had hung on the wall to make the room my own, but now they only mocked me. I saw my possessions strewn all over the floor because I no longer had the strength to clean up after myself.

I was looking for, I don't know, something to call my bluff. Some reason to stop me from doing what I was about to do. I could not even find one reason to stay my execution.

Honestly, I have no idea what I was looking for. I only saw the cold white walls and the hard-tiled floor, offering no comfort, reassurance, or anything. I was looking for a reason to keep fighting, but at the same time, I knew in my heart that I was too far gone. Nothing was going to stop me from the necessary evil that was waiting in my hand.

It's funny; only in my final minutes could I see every mistake I made so clearly and what had led me to this moment. Again and again, I relived every mistake with such perfect clarity that I could see how I could have avoided each one. Yet, it was too late; I did not care anymore. It felt like nothing more could be taken from me. The fight that had been inside me for so long and that had gotten me through so much was gone. Like a candle in the wind, it was blown out. I knew I was beaten down and ready to ring the final bell.

My failures, amplified and stacked on top of each other, still played like a bad movie in my mind. I looked down at the knife lying in my hand, but through my tear-streaked eyes, I did not see a blade. I saw a way out, a tool for finding the sleep I so severely needed. With my whole world burning down around me, I only had one more card to play, and I was more than ready to use it. I looked around the room and let the anger course through me. A joyless smile crossed my face. It was ironic. The last thing I would look at before I found my peace was a place I hated and the site of my worst mistakes, mistakes that would never be undone. With a heavy heart, I raised the tool of my freedom and started the downward plunge. Ready to meet nothing else but darkness.

My life did flash before my eyes in the final minutes. But the funny thing is, I did not see what I expected. I thought I would be watching my greatest triumphs and my most profound losses. Instead, I saw the lessons I had learned over the years. I saw the truths I found in life and the experiences I went through to understand them. I saw not my crowning achievements, but rather the ideas that helped me reach those achievements. In what I thought to be my final moments, I saw every reason I had ever fallen to the ground, and I saw every reason I was able to get back off the mat, dust myself off, and keep fighting.

2 WORTH FIGHTING FOR

I am sitting in class during my tenth-grade year, and the teacher just posed a question.

"What is the reason you get out of bed every morning? What drives you to start a new day? What's inside that tells you it is time to start fresh again?"

I thought about this and had a response in my mind, but I did not raise my hand. Everyone else was deep in thought, and hands started to rise. One answer was given.

"The reason is purely biological. Getting out of bed is just the brain telling the body it needs to do certain things to survive. It is purely animal instincts. It all comes from the brain."

I heard this response and felt it was the wrong way to look at things. The answer did not make sense to me, yet I still did not raise my hand. At that point in my life, I was recovering from my fourth surgery and having a tough time overall. I struggled to keep up with my school assignments, had therapy multiple times a week, and felt isolated from everyone around me. During this time, I realized that the worst experience in the world is feeling alone despite being surrounded by people. To be honest, I was depressed. Every time I started to stand up again, life would throw another shitstorm at me. I just felt so tired and done with everything.

I would get up every morning and try to keep pushing forward, yet I did not know what kept me going. It seemed beyond reason, yet every morning, I would get up and start my day regardless of how I felt. I knew something deep inside me was still fighting for my life, but I did not know what it was. Every morning, it was like I had a battle inside my head. On one side, there were many reasons to give up. But on the other side was this lone soldier who would continue fighting and keep me on the straight and narrow. I don't know how, but that lone fighter won victory after victory. Yet I did not even know the name of this warrior who would fight a pitched battle for me each morning.

Finally, I raised my hand, an infrequent occurrence for me. I am usually very closed off and prefer to avoid drawing attention to myself. I have always been content to share as little as possible about myself and give to others as much as possible. Maybe it is because I never wanted to draw attention to my CP; if people were not looking at me, they would not see my disability. I guess that was my thinking. But, this time, for whatever reason, I needed to say what was on my mind. I raised my hand and gave my answer.

"I don't know what drives someone to get out of bed each morning," I said. "But I know from my experiences that it is much deeper than just my brain telling me it is time to get up; it is way more than animal instinct. I am going through a lot right now, and it is my brain that wants me to end it all, and it is my brain that wants to make the pain go away. My brain is telling me that I would be better off dead. Yet, something deep inside announces that I will get out of bed every morning and try again. A feeling deep within gives me the much-needed push to get out of bed every morning and start my day. If it were only up to my brain, I would still be in bed right now, feeling like crap. Or, in the worst case, I would not be alive right now. I must believe it is more than just my brain telling me to start the day because if I stop believing, I know I have lost the battle, and I should just stop trying. I do not know what calls to me and makes me start my day, but I damn sure know it is not my brain. It needs to be something much deeper than that; it just has to be. I need it to be."

Listening to the stunned silence after speaking, I could not believe what I had said. I'd let something slip that I promised myself I would never say. I had divulged how unhappy, beaten down, and broken I felt. I had broken an unspoken rule and could do nothing about it. As soon as the words were out of my mouth, I wanted to find a way to put them back in, but I could not. They were now out in the universe for everyone to hear.

I looked around the room and felt like I had just made the biggest mistake of my life. A few seconds after I finished my speech, the bell for the next class mercifully rang. I made a quick exit and tried to avoid eye contact with everybody.

But as I was walking through the hallway, people were coming up to me and patting me on the shoulder, and everyone was telling me they were happy I shared. They said it showed the strength of my character to be able and willing share something like that with everyone. I could not believe it. What I saw as a mistake, others were taking as a sign of my strength. At that moment, I could not appreciate what that truly meant. A couple of years later, I fully perceived the impact of answering that question.

I am in twelfth grade. Near the end of the year, the entire school gathered for a weekend to celebrate the end of the year and give a send-off to the senior class as we moved toward our futures. It was a time of celebration. For me, this moment meant a couple of things. First, it marked that I had finally reached the end of my high school career, which was a big deal. With everything I had to deal with during my four years, I never imagined this day would arrive. Second, I would move to New York to attend college in a few months. This was huge for me; it would be the first time I was living on my own. It was scary, but exciting. Lastly and most importantly, I would finally understand something that would help me live my best life. I just did not know it yet.

At one point during the weekend, the teacher in charge of all the activities spoke to each of us seniors individually. It was like his closing words to each of us. It was an emotionally charged atmosphere. I was the first that he spoke to. The words he gave me have had a lasting impact on my life; it was as if his speech to me was the final piece of a puzzle I had been trying to finish ever since I answered that question two years ago. I had known this teacher since I was in sixth grade; he knew me well and all the struggles I had been through. Over the years, we had grown close, which made his words even more impactful. He looked me straight in the eyes and said:

"As long as I have known you, you have gone to hell and back more times than I can count. Your life has not always been easy, yet I never heard you complain about it once. The most impressive thing to me is that after everything you have gone through, every time I see you, you have a great big smile on your face no matter what. No matter how bad things may get, you always try to stay happy and put others before yourself. That is something exceptional. Always remember never, never to give up."

At first, I did not grasp the full implications of these words; I thought his speech meant that he was proud of me and everything I had accomplished despite my disability. It seemed like he was congratulating me on how well I could handle each obstacle that had come my way. I could not have been farther from the truth. I suddenly felt tears streaming down my face. I thought, "Crap, I do not want people to see me crying." But I looked around the room after he finished talking and noticed that my eyes were not the only wet ones. My classmates were also crying. At first, I did not understand why, but it all became apparent.

A lightbulb had been turned on in my head. There was only one explanation for why my friends were crying alongside me. I never wanted anything more than to prove I could get past anything life had to throw at me. However, while accomplishing that goal, I did something I never suspected I would do. I had not only gained the support of my teachers and friends, but I had also gained their respect. I finally knew the name of that lone soldier fighting for me. I now like to call it "something worth fighting for."

In times when I wanted to give up, I was never sure what kept me going until that weekend. I finally understood that I could only push myself off the floor repeatedly because I had something to strive for. Something that made what I went through hurt a little less and make a little more sense.

Even when I did not know it, I had friends behind me who supported me. In the back of my mind, even if I wanted to raise up the white flag, a part of me kept fighting because I had people in my corner who would have hated to see me give up. Even though I wanted to give up on myself occasionally, I knew in the back of my mind that I had people supporting me and cheering me on. It gave me something worth fighting for. Without knowing it, I had one reason never to back down and to push myself forward little by little. I had a reason to keep fighting for myself.

I have learned that life is not always going to be easy. It is just a fact that you will get knocked on your ass more times than you can count. In those moments, you feel like the world's weight is pushing down on you. All the odds might be against you, but I promise, just like me, you still have that soldier in your head pushing you forward and helping you get through every day. That brave little warrior is, as I like to call it, something worth fighting for. It is something that you may not even know is there. However, it is hard at work for you. It will give you the push you always need to keep moving forward.

What does "something worth fighting for" really mean?

That is not easy to answer because it is something different for everyone. For a long time, I did not even know what it was for me. However, I can tell you what it feels like when you find it. For me, at least, it means finding something that puts a fire, a passion, in your body and soul. It is a feeling that washes over you and gives you a sense of purpose. It is the one thing that, time and time again, will always give you the motivation to never give up. Every obstacle you encounter makes more sense because, for the first time, you can see that bigger things are at play. When found, it becomes your mission in life. You want to live your life to the fullest when you find something worth fighting for. Come high or hell water, you will always want to keep this feeling in your heart.

Like me, you can find something worth fighting for and not even know it. Yet, it will be there in the back of your mind. It is keeping you standing on your feet. Even if you feel beyond broken, that soldier will be there, telling you not to give up on yourself. Once you can identify and name what you are fighting for, it will be like a new world opens for you. It will be like the final piece of the puzzle coming into place. Just like me, you will understand that the purpose you just found will help you fight long after you want to quit.

I keep using the phrase "something worth fighting for," but another way of putting it would be "leaving an impact." Finding something worth fighting for and making an impact are the same. They have the same goal: finding a way to make this earth seem a little brighter and a little better each day. Yet, an impact is so much more than just leaving a mark to show that you were here. It can have a domino effect. It can inspire hope, and hope is a powerful thing.

This is wild to think about. Just by finding something you believe in and being determined to enhance the world around you, you leave something long-lasting in this world. The piece of you that is left behind can change the lives of everyone around you for years to come. When you are long gone, your impact will inspire people to make the same choices you made. You can start a chain reaction to move the world into a brighter tomorrow.

Finding something you want to fight for gives you a purpose. It is with that purpose that you can start making your impact. The goal you see does not come from your brain; it comes from deep inside of you. It is something you feel in your whole body. When your purpose is in your mind, it fills you with hope for the future. When you want to make an impact you care deeply about, nothing can stand in your way. Every time you get pushed to the ground think about why you keep fighting, and your purpose, and I promise you will be able to laugh it off like it is nothing.

Without even knowing it, I was doing this all the time. Every time I was knocked down, and believe me, there were many, it was the purpose I had deep inside that would help me back on my feet and keep me moving in the right direction. Even if I wanted to give up on myself, there was no way in hell I was going to disappoint the people cheering for me.

Sometimes, I was too blinded by my pain to see my impact on others. I think that happens many times in a person's life. You can have so much on your plate that you forget to step back. When my teacher spoke to me that weekend, it was my chance to take a step back. Only when I could look at everything, did I finally I see what I was fighting for. I could not see the bigger picture; that is the essential point.

When life seems like an endless tunnel of hardships, we tend to look at what is right before us. Naturally, it is easier to think small. Yet, this fallacy makes it seem like hard times are the only things in the world. Only when you have something worth fighting for, an impact to make, can you stop thinking small and look at everything as a whole. Having something worth fighting for gives you a light to hold in your darkest moments. The fire in your soul will always guide you out of the dark and back into the light. It gives you a reason to look at your future and never want to give up. Always keep holding on to the knowledge that you have a difference to make; it will always guide you to the path you want to be on.

When I was able to look at the bigger picture, I understood I had to keep going. If not for my sake, then for the sake of my friends and family, who were always in my corner cheering me on. I knew what I was fighting for, and I knew that I still had an impact to make. When I discovered why I had always kept fighting, I also found what I could give to this world. Not to sound too conceited, but I could be someone people looked to for inspiration. I could become a character of hope. I feel like I can inspire people; at least, I hope I can.

When you feel like you want to give up, I don't know; maybe I can be the reason you keep fighting. All these thoughts ran through my head when my teacher finished talking to me. It was one of the best things that ever happened to me. For the first time in my life, events that happened to me started to make sense and I knew I had done things the right way. Now, when I look back on that time, answering that question and hearing what my teacher had to say, I know those expcricnces gave me a gift I would never trade for anything: the ability to look deep within myself and remember what I am made of.

This is the true magic of finding something worth fighting for. It can lead you to places you never thought you would be. It will give you the courage to push yourself off the ground. Finding something worth fighting for leads you to a purpose; with that purpose, you can start making an impact.

At the heart of it, having something you are willing to fight for gives you the strength you need. With that strength, you will never give up, because it means there are still significant changes you want to make within your life. As I said before, having something worth fighting for gives you a candle to hold in your darkest moments. I hope that when that candle is lit for you, it means just as much as it did for me. Always fight for what you want because that is the only way you will ever impact this world.

So, I have a question for you. What are you fighting for?

3 MOMENTS

I am six years old, and having my second surgery. It had only been a year since my first one, and I was frightened all over again. I could not believe I needed to have another one so close to the first. It felt like someone was playing a cruel joke on me, and believe me, I was not laughing. Since no one was jumping out of a closet and saying, "gotcha," I knew I had to come to terms with my fate. I felt like my childhood was being ripped away from me and I was forced to grow up too fast. But mainly, I was scared.

I only knew what the first surgery was like, and I thought this one would be the same. I remembered every feeling from the first operation. The pain, the fear, the hours of rehab, but most of all, I remembered the exhaustion. I did not know if I could go through all that again. However, I already understood that if I suffered now, my future self would thank me. Ready or not, I finally came to terms with another surgery.

I did my best to prepare, yet in the back of my mind, there was still that worm of fear regarding what would be thrown my way. I knew all I could do was try to get to the other side of this challenge the best I could; the problem was that I did not know how. I was only six; how was I supposed to deal with a challenge of this magnitude? From this young age, I learned something vital. Challenges were always going to come my way, regardless of my age. I could only face each obstacle on the battlefield and try my best; this surgery would have to be no different.

The day of the surgery arrived. As we got to the hospital, I felt like the weight of the world was sitting on my chest. However, I did not show it. I thought if I projected calmness, then maybe I would be calm. I was very wrong. While we were waiting, a nurse asked me if I wanted something to calm me down so it would be easier to get the surgical mask on me for the anesthesia.

I said no because I was still trying to act calm; that was my next mistake. That day, I learned that one of the bravest things I could ever do was always be honest about my feelings. Unfortunately, I realized that when it was a little too late. On the operating table, as the doctors were putting the mask on me, my fear suddenly overtook me. I would not let them put it on me. It felt like the walls were closing in, and it became a struggle.

It took a while, but when the mask was finally on and I started feeling the effects of the medicine, a sense of calmness washed over me. I closed my eyes, getting ready to fall asleep. Even with my eyes closed, I could still see my parents standing over me in my mind's eye, wishing me good luck, even though I knew they had left the operating room some minutes earlier. However, the picture was crystal clear in my mind. At that moment, seeing my parents in my mind, I knew everything would be okay. It was as if all my fear melted away at that moment, and all I was left with was utter calmness.

I am in high school, and I have a friendship with the security guard. Every week, we make bets on football games. We designed the stakes to make fun of the losing party—things like bowing to the winner or singing to him. Even though the bets were for small things, they meant a lot to us. As the games got more important, the stakes got more humiliating. But neither of us, in fact, found it embarrassing because these little wagers brought us fun and laughter.

In one game, we made a bet that whenever the losing party saw the victor, he had to walk around like a duck, making quacking sounds and flapping his hands. I lost, and gave my duck impression whenever I saw him.

I ate with everybody in the hallway that day. While I was with my friends, the guard stopped by. So, I stopped eating, and in front of everyone in the hall, I became a duck, quacking, flapping my arms, bobbing my head, the whole nine yards. Everyone who saw my performance was laughing and having a good time. While giving my routine, I looked around the hall, and all I saw were smiling faces. I instantly felt pride because I knew I made their smiles possible. It was at this time that a profound idea hit me.

I learned the power of making people happy. Not only was I able to be part of a good time, but I also created a moment of joy for the others around me. I learned to never underestimate the gift of making a moment for others. Another lesson I learned that day is that if you are okay with making a fool of yourself, you can always have a good time. At that moment, I was quacking like a duck. I was not embarrassed.

I understood that if I hadn't transformed into a duck, I would have missed out on a moment I now treasure forever. Once I could get out of my head and not care what other people thought about me, I was the happiest I had ever been. I could only live for truly great moments when I freed myself from the fear of standing out. My CP makes it so that I naturally stand out. For many years, this bothered me. But at this moment, I figured I would stand out anyway. I might use it to my advantage and make people laugh. Standing out will never be wrong if I can make use of it and bring joy to others.

I am twenty. I am recovering from yet another surgery, and worries about my future are on my mind. My future needed to be more focused. I was at a fork in the road of my life, and I did not know which way to turn. During this time, the football playoffs were happening. Some friends I didn't get to see that often were in town. I texted one of them and asked if he and the others wanted to come over and watch the game. He said they had some stuff to do first and would try to come over during the fourth quarter, which they did. It was a great time, watching football with my friends and catching up.

At that moment, it did not matter that I was dealing with surgery, and I did not care about my future. I let all my worries melt away and enjoyed my time with them. During that quarter, all that was asked of me was to enjoy the game and the time I had with my friends. Nothing else mattered but enjoying the moment. Even though it only lasted a few minutes, when I look back on that time, I do not think about how I was recovering from surgery or how uncertain my future was. What I remember is the fun I had with my friends.

I have learned that life moves pretty fast, and funny enough, the more you try to slow it down, the quicker time seems to go. I sometimes think that going through life and experiencing it are two separate things. I get so focused on the struggles in my life, and I soon realize that it is just passing me by. It feels like I am taking a back seat and watching my life go by in the rearview mirror. The more I hold on to what I think is essential, the more I lose out on the times that actually matter.

But now I think I know how to rectify that problem. I have learned that there will always be hard times. Unfortunately, there is no way around it. But I now know that life is not measured in time; it is counted by the moments that make it worth all the ups and downs.

Time moves in a funny manner; when you want it to slow down, it seems lightning fast, and when you want time to speed up, it tends to move at a snail's pace. When it comes down to it, there never seems to be enough of it for anything. But time is not what we should be after; what matters are those moments that can be found within time.

I was very angry for the longest time because I felt cheated out of my time. Many hardships marked my childhood and adolescence. It was as if that time in my life was ripped away from me, and for many years, I was angry. That was until I understood that it was not how much time I had that mattered, but how many moments I could make in my life. Moments, for me, mean something that alters my understanding of what is happening around me. Only when I started living in these moments could I start living my life to the fullest.

It took me a long time to learn that there are two kinds of moments. Most moments are brief, and all that is asked of you is to be happy. A moment is an unplanned stop in your day to spend with friends and family. It provides you with time to enjoy yourself despite whatever may be happening in your life. For a short time, you can forget all about your worries, and that is a beautiful thing.

Watching the football game with my friends and paying my debt to the security guard are just examples of how great moments can be. Moments like that are when you can let go, laugh, and enjoy yourself. Those are the moments that will always matter the most. I promise you, no matter how much time you have, if it is filled with beautiful moments that bring a smile to your face, your life will be a good one.

However, I do not want to lie to you. There is another kind of moment that comes and leaves you cold and feeling alone. It can turn your life into ashes. This moment will come out of nowhere and make you feel like you are in a living hell. Yet these bad moments are as important as the good ones. In life, you cannot have good without evil. But by the same token, the bad can never overshadow the good. You will have bad moments, but all they do in the long run is enhance how you enjoy the good moments.

Both of these events are called moments for a reason. Because they do not last, they are all the more special—that is their very nature. A joyous moment must be cherished for what it is: fleeting. It takes you out of your daily routine and gives you a chance to relax and enjoy the life you have. Instantly, it is gone, and you're back to the regularly scheduled program.

But moments can be found multiple times a day if you look hard enough. In the morning, having coffee with loved ones; in the afternoon, taking a break with coworkers and friends; and at night, having dinner with your family are just a few examples, but there are many more to be found if you look. Knowing there are so many moments makes it easier to let one go when it is done because you know another is around the corner, just waiting to be found. Knowing that moments are brief makes dealing with the challenging ones easier. You know they will not last forever. The pain will eventually end, and you can start looking forward to the joyous moments in life again.

The joy you get from moments can give you the strength required to accomplish anything you want. A moment is beautiful on its own, yet it can also have a second level.

Let me paint you a picture. You wake up late because your alarm did not go off. While driving to work, you spill coffee all over yourself. This is a lousy way to start the day, but at the office, it gets worse. When you arrive, your boss yells at you for being late because you had to drive home and change clothes. You finally get to your desk and realize you forgot a crucial file you need at home. From that point on, it is a miserable morning. You finally get a break in the day and time for lunch, but here comes the boss, who tells you that you need to work through lunch to redo the paperwork you forgot. It takes the rest of the afternoon to finish the work; you drive home in a bad mood.

What scene are you met with when you walk in the front door? Your daughter waits by the entrance to hug you and ask if you will play with her. An hour later, you are dressed as a princess and having a tea party. The moment you spend with your daughter makes your trying day seem like nothing more than a speck on the radar of what matters.

The true magnificence of the good moments is that they are hope wrapped up in a box. I believe that beautiful moments and hope have the same address. When swimming through the crap that can be life sometimes, these moments sprinkle joy and tell you to take a breath and enjoy yourself.

Moments of any kind help remind you that you are only on this earth for a limited time. With that in mind, let me ask you a question. What do you want to focus on? Horrible times that take away from your joy, or all the moments that give you pleasure?

I want to be in the moments of happiness as much as possible. It is all too easy to get bogged down by the moments of hardship in life. Yet, if you open yourself up to all the fantastic moments around you, they can eclipse the crummy moments when they happen. You are only here for a short time. So, could you make the most of it? Let me tell you a secret: Things always have a way of working themselves out. Free your mind of all the things that cause you pain; I promise you, they are not worth it. Please spend your time in the moments that make you smile, because those moments will stick with you forever.

Life moves pretty fast. Your job is to get as much as possible out of it before it is gone. You do that by living in each moment that gives you joy—soaking in every second of it and allowing yourself to be happy. When you find you are in a happy moment, take the time to breathe it in and enjoy it. It will be gone in the blink of an eye, but that means more to come. I promise you, if you put in the time to look for each fantastic moment, you will find them. It helps if you also remember that the bad moments will end. You just have to stick them out.

So, let me leave you with a challenge. Look for the great moments whenever you can. Enjoy the hell out of it when you find one. Because after all is said and done, moments of any type make life worth living.

4 THE CONTENDERS

Sitting up on the stage at graduation was one of the proudest moments of my life. I had worked and fought so hard for this day. I could not believe it was finally here. I was suddenly overtaken with powerful emotions. For many years, it had felt like graduation was for other people, but not me. But suddenly I was here.

Honestly, I felt like this was owed to me. Every day, I tried not to feel like I was entitled to anything, but damn it, I thought I had more than earned this. Passing on from high school showed that no matter what shit was thrown my way, I could overcome any obstacle. Despite my hardship, I was able to still focus on my education and excel. On that stage, I thought back to everything that had transpired during the last four years.

Right off the bat, high school did not start as I wanted. A year before ninth grade, I knew I would have surgery in the summer leading up to the first day of school. So, my whole eighth-grade year consisted of anxiety about the upcoming surgery and how that would affect my education. The two months before school started were spent trying to rehab the best I could. However, I was still recovering when the first day arrived, and I could not make it a full day at first because I would tire too quickly.

As a result, I began to fall behind in my schoolwork, which only added to my exhaustion. Fortunately, my school understood what I was going through and the staff was kind enough to tell me to get in each assignment when I could. This did make the situation more manageable, but there was still a lot on my plate. Throughout it all, I kept having one repeating thought: Why did I have to go through this? Let me tell you, when no answer was given, I started to falter. But at the same time, this was only my first year of high school. Surely things would get better, right?

No, I was wrong. My second year of high school started the same way my first did: The summer preceding tenth grade, I needed another surgery. Yet again, the staff at my school understood my situation and was very accommodating. I could not believe what was happening to me. I had just finished recovering from one surgery and now had to do it again. I was angry, and honestly, I was depressed. It felt like my time in high school was being taken away from me.

However, there was a silver lining. I knew I was not having surgery the summer that preceded eleventh grade. Finally, after two years of hell, I would have a typical summer, and for the first time in a long time, I would feel like a typical teenager. This was going to be my summer and my year. I told myself I would have the high school experience I always wanted.

But luck was not with me. A week before school started, I injured myself and needed surgery to repair the damage. Three years of surgeries in a row, what the hell? If that was not bad enough, lousy luck struck again while I was recovering from this most recent surgery. I injured myself again and needed yet another surgery a few months after the last one. I was getting body blow after body blow and could never throw a punch of my own.

Senior year arrived. I was waiting for the other shoe to drop, and it did. I passed the summer, passed the first couple weeks of school. But one day, I woke up with my back in spasms. From that day on, for the next two and a half months, I was in terrible pain and barely able to move, making me miss a chunk of my twelfth-grade year. So, my high school career was different from what I wanted it to be. Through four long years, not only did I deal with surgeries, but I also dealt with pain, too many hours of physical therapy, and battles with depression.

All of this flashed through my mind as I was graduating. Let me be honest; I only remember a little about my graduation. However, the one part I know I will remember till the end of my days was when the principal called my name, and I went up to accept my diploma. At that moment, everything I had been through just felt like an afterthought. I realized that I'd crushed every challenge that had come my way and kept moving forward, and that was all that mattered. After four years of feeling like my life was out of control, I would finally have total control. The independence people search for in high school always felt like a pipe dream. Something I always wanted yet would never have. At that moment, touching my diploma for the first time, I realized it was finally within my reach.

It was my time to shine. For as long as I can remember, I have felt overshadowed by my condition. But I understood that was how it needed to be. The CP demanded certain things of me, which I had to accept. I had to put aside what I wanted, and I did what I needed. As hard as it was, I knew I needed to sacrifice some of my childhood for my later life to improve. Trust me, I was not too fond of it, but I understood what was required of me. Most of the time, it hurt like hell, but I always knew it would be worth it in the future. However, the future was finally here; this time I would be in control of my life. Going to college in New York was going to be a turning point. I could not have been more excited.

Buying everything I would need and packing up all my stuff felt like such an adventure. Each item purchased and packed felt like one step closer to a future I'd never thought would be mine. For months, I had been in contact with the teachers and faculty of the college I would attend. After many conversations, all the accommodations I would need were set up.

To make the transition into college life a little easier, I had one of the career counselors set up my class schedule. I sent her an email telling her what I was interested in and what I wanted my major to be, and she sent a class schedule according to those guidelines. Without even realizing it, I was relinquishing some of the control I so desperately wanted just because I wanted to make my life a little easier. But I did not understand that at the time.

With all my bags packed, I was finally ready to embark on my future. My father was going to bring me to New York and help me get everything set up in my dorm room. Traveling to the airport and getting through security was all a blur. Yet, taking that first step onto the airplane was surreal. It was as if everything in my life had been leading up to this point. All the pain, the depression, and the sacrifices I had made were all for this moment.

I wanted to pause time and understand what this truly meant to me. Honestly, stepping onto that plane was so significant for me. It was a testament to who I was and what I wanted to become. I did it, and I passed every obstacle thrown my way. I was the victor of every battle I had to fight. I may have been battered and bruised, but I never once gave up; there were many times I wanted to but never did.

Through it all, I fought for a future I could never imagine but hoped was out there somewhere. Now that future was finally here. I could not believe it. I found my seat on the plane and saw my life ahead of me. The airplane took off, and with that, I left the past behind me. I was off to a new, exciting chapter.

5 INNER STRENGTH

I am in the last week of summer break, entering my eleventh-grade year. I am in my kitchen, cleaning up after my lunch. I am holding a glass cup in my right hand in the process of taking it to the sink. I stumble and fall. As I hit the ground, the cup shatters in my hand.

At first, lying on the floor, I did not think anything was wrong. However, as I started moving my right hand, I saw blood gushing on the floor. My family came in, and my brother helped me get up. The kitchen floor looked like a murder scene. I dared a glance at my hand, and the sight sent shivers down my spine. A massive laceration started between my thumb and index finger and went all the way to just before the start of my palm. With panic, I realized I had no sensation in half my hand. Which, in retrospect, was probably a good thing because I did not feel the glass slicing through it.

We wrapped my hand and went to the emergency room. The nurses put me on a bed and immediately wheeled me into an examination room. They took an x-ray because they feared that glass shards were left in my hand. With that done, a doctor came in to start stitching me up. The room looked like a bloodbath had taken place. The injury would not stop bleeding. My hand was numbed so the needle could go in, but my body was metabolizing the medicine too quickly. So, I had to get five rounds of the numbing medication. As each shot went in, I could feel it somewhat, but not totally.

Finally, my hand was stitched up, but I was told I would need to see a hand specialist to determine the amount of damage. That night, I found it very hard to sleep. I still had feeling in half of my hand, and that half was hurting like hell. Eventually, I was able to get somewhat comfortable and get some sleep.

The following day, I woke to find that my hand had started bleeding again at some point in the night. My mother was prepared to take me to the emergency room again; however, when the nurse for the hand specialist called, she told my mother to bring me into his office instead. It was a godsend that we did not have to deal with the emergency room a second time. The specialist looked at my hand and told me I would have surgery to repair my nerves and fix the damage. I could not believe what I was hearing. I went from thinking I would not have any surgery this school year to having one just four days before it was about to start.

Fortunately, four days did not give me much time to think about what I would once again be facing. So, I had another surgery. As soon as it was over, I knew it had been a success because I felt the most unbearable pain in my hand, meaning the nerves had been repaired. It felt like a hundred knives were stabbing into it simultaneously. However, knowing the alternative, I was happy to feel the pain. Luckily, the recovery was not long. I was back at school just a few days after the operation.

My rehab was going well; my hand was now in a splint, and I was on my way to being fully recovered. Then I hit a bump in the road. Seven months after the surgery, I was out with my mom and sister when I tripped and fell on my splint. As soon as I fell, I knew something was wrong because I was in more pain than before. Once again, we were in the emergency room, where the ER doctor told me I had broken my thumb. Also, since it was the hand that I had just had surgery on, I needed to see the hand specialist again.

The hand specialist presented some unwelcome news. Not only had I broken a bone in my thumb, but I had ripped it out of the thumb entirely. So, I would need another surgery to remove the bone and fix my thumb. I just sat there dumbfounded. Two surgeries in the span of seven months; it was just insane to think about. Yet, I knew this was reality, so I just had to suck it up and get through another operation.

I will not lie to you; my strength was tested. It was a hard time for me, but it was also an informative point in my life. I felt like I had hit rock bottom. How in the hell would I make it through another recovery when I was still rehabbing from a surgery that took place less than a year before?

It felt like I kept getting sucker punched. It felt like my back was against the wall. I thought back to everything I had already been through in my life and how I had overcome every challenge that had been put in my path. All the periods of my life when I felt like I was beaten, and how each of those times I found the strength I needed to keep pushing on. Those thoughts filled me with the courage I needed to overcome this obstacle.

This whole episode enlightened me about the power of having inner strength. I had been through hard times before and had to dig deep within myself. But this was the first time I finally knew what I was digging into. Physical strength is one thing, but inner strength is another ball of yarn. Having inner strength, at least for me, means having the power and motivation to keep going long after you want to give up. Inner strength is when you get the shit kicked out of you, and still, you are willing to put a smile back on your face and try to keep moving forward.

Look, I am going to tell you something you already know. Life is hard, and anyone who tells you otherwise is lying. Anything worth having in this world requires strength from within. Being strong, both physically and mentally, is a must in this life. But it has been my experience that power and inner strength are very different. I have always been strong, and I needed to be. For a long time, that was enough. But later in life, I found I needed something more. Having inner strength is almost like being stubborn. It is being stubborn enough to never let anything get the way of what you want out of your life.

I realized that bull-rushing through every obstacle would not be enough anymore. Then, I discovered my inner strength. When you look deep inside, you will find that you have immense reserves of strength you didn't know about. When you realize you have this inner fortitude, you can call upon it when you are in need. It will come to you in your darkest times. When you feel defeated, your inner strength will light a fire to guide you back to who you once were. With this power, you can climb out of the deepest depths of your hell and continue moving forward.

At times in my life, I felt like everything was against me. I felt like I had hit the lowest point, but deep inside me, a voice was screaming to me and still willing to fight on my behalf. That was my inner strength, an ever-present voice telling me to keep going. It is a voice that pushes me to be my best and gets me through my darkest moments.

When you have a dream, life tests you to see how much it is worth. This is where inner strength comes in. You must plant your feet firmly on the ground and tell life that it can throw everything it wants at you, but you are not moving and will not give up on your dreams. Your strength, deep within, will give you the resolve needed to accomplish anything you want. However, having that kind of fortitude does so much more for you. Not only did my inner strength help me get through some hard times, but it also gave me the confidence to know the certainty of life. Yes, there will be times when I feel like all the odds are against me. But I must always have the courage to stand tall in the eye of the hurricane. Inner strength will allow you to withstand anything and help you keep moving forward. Your inner strength will always help you battle for what you want most.

One of the beautiful things about inner strength is that you have it even if you do not know about it. You just need the fortitude to use it. I mostly found myself in extreme situations, either sink or swim, and that's how I found my inner strength. Yet everyone is different; you will find your strength differently, but only if you are willing to do the work. Inner strength gives you the ability to change the world. But on the other side, if you are not brave enough, it will be left untapped and forever forgotten. Audacity is required if you want to access its full power. You need to have the courage to look at the world and say that it can and should be better.

Inner strength is the one thing that can never be broken. When your life feels like endless hardships and every other part of you feels broken down, I promise that the strength inside you is the one part that remains whole. Even when you feel like life is burning down around you, the power you have inside is hard at work, repairing everything piece by piece. Once you're back up, inner strength will give you the fortitude to look life straight in the eyes and say, "Is that all you got?"

With every obstacle you overcome, your inner strength increases. Like any other muscle, the more you use it, the stronger it gets. The more powerful your inner strength gets, the more obstacles you can overcome. Having inner strength does not just happen, you must tap into this stubbornness. Every time an obstacle comes your way, imagine it is a workout to improve your inner strength. The more you defy the odds, the stronger your inner strength gets.

To simplify what inner strength means, let me use a different term: courage. Courage helps you get off the floor every time, all the time. Everything you want in this world requires courage. Having courage means knowing that better things are on the horizon. When you find yourself in rough seas, you must have the strength to fight tooth and nail to get to calmer waters. Sometimes, all it takes is just one courageous act to change the course of your history. One second where you put all your strength on the line. Just one final push.

Your courage always comes to you when you need it the most. When the walls are crumbling down, your inner strength takes over and helps you do precisely what is required to come out the other side stronger than before. With courage on your side, anything is possible, and there are no limits to what you can achieve. When you put your courage on the line like that, I promise, you will never be disappointed. Every single damn surgery took all my courage, and every time I was rewarded.

Courage is a strange beast sometimes. It is not just something you can say you have; you must prove you have it. It is not enough to say you will be courageous. You can say you have it all you want, but you can only prove it when the shit hits the fan. I have learned that courage is not always some spectacular act of heroism. It does not need to involve unfathomable physical strength. No, sometimes the most courageous act is admitting how you feel. It can be the quiet act of just showing up. You never know if that kind of courage might save your life someday.

Inner strength and courage are two sides of the same coin. In essence, both are a declaration of your desire to never give up on yourself. When I dug deep and found the strength to recover from two surgeries only months apart, I was calling on my inner strength, my courage, or whatever you want to call it.

The point is that you can make a declaration of your own. You can call on what is deep within to give you the power to pursue your dreams. So, I guess there is only one question left: How much courage do you have to chase your dreams?

6 ACCEPTING YOU FOR YOU

I am in my third-grade year. I have already undergone two surgeries and countless different procedures. I am well versed in what comes along with my disability.

However, at that time in my life, I was not well versed in interacting with my friends or understanding how I wanted them to interact with me. It felt like there was an invisible wall blocking me from them. I had felt this way for a long time and did not know what to do about it. As a third grader, I already understood that because of the nature of my disability, I would always stand out. As a young child, this bothered me. But I knew I had to get familiar with the feeling quickly. To learn how to go about doing that, I was going to need some help.

I talked to the school's learning specialist. It was the right move. She suggested that maybe my friends were cautious toward me because they did not understand what CP was. Perhaps if they learned more about it and how it affected me, the wall would start to crumble. She suggested I make a presentation explaining my condition, the best way for my friends to act around me, and how I wanted to be treated.

I thought this was a great idea and believed it would help. At the same time, I had some apprehension. This would be the first time that I would be actively talking about my disability, and I was not sure if I was ready for that. What if my classmates made fun of me? What if this presentation led to more problems and a deeper divide between me and my peers? Would the project have the outcome I wanted, or would it be a disaster? I had no idea. This was a big step for me, but somehow, I knew I had to take it regardless of the outcome. Good or bad, this was something I needed to do for myself.

For weeks, the special ed teacher and I worked on the presentation, with help from one of my best friends I had grown up with. Even though I had my concerns, I put my heart and soul into the presentation. In my head, there were two possible outcomes. One, this would not help; if anything, it would make it even more apparent how different I was from my peers. It could make me feel all the more isolated—which scared me.

But I also saw another outcome that filled me with hope. My project would be a huge success. My friends would enjoy it and learn a lot about who I was. I could make more significant relationships with my classmates and feel like I was not so different or so alone. I could feel normal; I would start to feel like part of the class. If others learned about me, I could feel comfortable with my identity. If I only had an idea of how successful my presentation would be and what I was about to set in motion.

The project was ready after a month and a half of hard work. I had a time set up to give the presentation. As I waited for the room to fill, I was surprised to see that more than just my classmates were taking their seats. Faculty and other staff were coming in as well. As an extra surprise, I saw my parents and grandmother coming in. It was such a pleasant shock to see everyone who had shown up. Suddenly, I felt a catch in my throat; I did not realize how much it meant for me to have so many people come and support me. Everyone entered and took their seats; it became silent. I took a deep breath. This was it; it was showtime.

I started slow and nervous. I went through each slide of the powerpoint. I detailed what my disability is, what my day-to-day life is like, the kind of equipment I have to use (like a wheelchair and leg braces), some of my interests (like what my favorite sports are), and how I would like my classmates to act around me. Accompanying the presentation was a video showing my classmates how I learned to fall. I explained that if I fell: I did not want them to help me up automatically, but I would like them to ask if I was okay and if I needed anything.

After I finished my presentation, I took a deep breath and asked if there were any questions. To my delight, hands started to go up It made me smile when my classmates wanted to know more about me and my condition. I thought this was where it would end, but I was very wrong.

The school asked if I would be willing to give my presentation to the other grades. I was more than happy after seeing the reaction from my class. So, over the next couple of months, I gave my presentation all over the school. This was an excellent experience for me. Not only was I educating the people around me, but I was also starting to accept my CP and who I was.

This presentation led me to places I never thought I would be. However, when I reflect on my time with the project, I never think about its success. I always think about how it started me on the long road of self-acceptance.

I am eighteen, and I am sitting at my graduation ceremony. It took a hell of a lot to get to this point, but I am finally here.

What I thought about myself before that point was inconsequential compared to what I learned that night. Throughout the evening, the principal of my school spoke to each student from the graduating class. When he talked to me, I knew it would be the closing of a chapter and the start of a new one. I waited excitedly for my name to be called.

Finally, my principal called me up; I stood from my chair and walked to where he was on the stage. His speech to me started much like the others before mine. He explained a little about me and my academics. But then he took a pause that felt like it lasted an eternity. He had not stopped like this in his other speeches. I was not prepared for what was coming next. I waited on pins and needles, yet the next thing out of his mouth was the last thing I expected.

"This is where this speech becomes a little bit difficult for me," he began. "As many of you know, David has some health challenges. However, he is far more than his health condition. I do not want to make this speech about his health; he deserves far more yet it would be not very responsible of me not to say what an inspiration he is to all who meet him. No matter what life has thrown at him. He is one of the most positive people around. His classmates describe him as an inspiration. I have never heard him complain about what he is going through; he is always the most positive person I have encountered on any given day. No matter what he is going through, his classmates say he always puts others first. When he attends college in New York next year, I know our halls will seem a little darker without him."

It felt like I had been blindsided but in a good way. The world flashed by me in slow motion as I heard those words. The next thing I knew, he handed me my diploma and took a picture. Walking back to my seat, I did not understand how to process what I had just heard.

But the night did not stop surprising me there. My next shock came toward the end of the ceremony. At this point, I was bored and just zoning out until I heard someone say my name. I looked up to see one of my classmates giving his graduation speech, and talking about how much he had learned in school.

"I have learned just as much from my friends as from the teachers," he said. "For instance, David came into our class in the first grade. To us, he was not the person in the wheelchair; he was the boy who never shied away from trying anything. He was a friend who embodied perseverance and grit. I do not think the students in this class look at people in wheelchairs or with other challenges quite the same after getting to know him, and I thank him for that."

Again, my world was flipped on its side. Two different people saw me just as I was. They did not see the CP. They saw a man with many different qualities who also happened to have CP. At this moment, I could fully accept myself for who I was. If other people could see me for myself, it was high time for me to do the same. It all hit me at once. Every time I had been in a challenging situation. Every time I had been battered and bruised and felt like I could not even take one more step. Somehow, I always did; it might have seemed beyond reason, yet, every single damn time, I was able to keep on fighting.

How and why? I had no idea for a long time, and I was okay without an explanation. All that mattered to me was that I was able to do it. It was not until graduation that I found out the reason. It was my CP. Time and time again, I only made it out of a complicated situation because my disability made me who I am. By the very nature of my CP, I was constantly overcoming obstacles. But my condition also made me strong enough to beat every challenge.

It doesn't sound straightforward, but I promise it is. Let me put it this way: I am nothing without my disability, and my disability is nothing without me. I am who I am because of my CP. It just took me a while to understand. When I was younger, I hated being disabled; it was like a blemish on my personality. It was a monkey on my back that I could never shake off. But now I understand something remarkable. Without my disability, a piece of who I am would be missing. I would not be as strong as I am, or as caring, if I did not have my CP. In short, I would not be me.

Yet, I am also so much more than just my disability. Not to pat myself too hard on the back, but I have been told I am intelligent, caring, perseverant, and funny, and that I put others first. These are great qualities, and just as they make me who I am, so too does my disability. All together, these are pieces of a picture that show the type of person I am and can become.

I am going to tell you straight out. You will only have a life once you accept yourself for who you are. However, this can be unpleasant because accepting who you are means standing alone and not just being part of the crowd. It means being comfortable in your own skin no matter what anyone else thinks. Maybe you feel like you must be a specific type of person to fit in. Because of this, you are under the impression that you must hide your true self to be like everybody else. I have felt that need many times myself.

A funny thing can happen, though; the longer you wear the "fake your costume," the more challenging it can be to take off. Over time, you begin to feel like it is the true you. The sad part is that eventually, down the road, you will not recognize yourself in the mirror. It is human nature to want to avoid standing out. Most of us would rather be just one in the crowd because it feels safer. But the person who can stand separate from the masses is the strongest. If you can be strong enough to accept yourself for who you are and stand alone, it will be one of the best things you ever do.

Trust me; I know this is easier said than done. It is always easier to live a lie than to live the truth. If you ever accept yourself for who you are, you must take the good and the bad. One thing most people avoid is admitting their shortcomings. However, I think "shortcomings" is a negative word that can make you believe the worst of yourself, and so it is the wrong word to use.

But what if you started to think differently? If you stop thinking about certain qualities as shortcomings and start looking at them as part of who you are and what makes you, you it will become much easier to accept who you are and be happy in your skin. There is no such thing as a shortcoming. There is only you and how you can make yourself that much better. So, accept who you are and grow every single day.

Everything you have is what makes you unique. There is, and there will only ever be, one you. So, do not waste time trying to fit into someone else mold. Use everything you have at your disposal to make your life a good one. I promise, if you try to live your life as part of a crowd, you will not have much of a life. When you accept who you are, you can start to look inward and see your personal idiosyncrasies not as shortcomings but as attributes to brighten up the world around you.

I know it can be scary to be who you are because of the worry that some people will not like what they see. But let me tell you something. You do not need to concern yourself with what people think about you. Nothing else matters as long as you are proud of who you are. It is not your job to try to make everyone like you; be yourself, and the people who matter the most will always accept the authentic you. If you constantly worry about what other people think, you will never be able to have a life.

Let me tell you a secret: No one cares about you. This might sound harsh, but I promise you it is not. Let me put it this way: While you are worried about what someone is thinking about you, that person is concerned about what you think about them. Meaning no one actually has the time to think about you. Once you realize no one is thinking about you, you can finally remove the "fake you costume." You can be free just to be yourself and enjoy your true self.

Acceptance is a long and hard road, but you must take it. You can start living once you can accept yourself, idiosyncrasies and all. You will have a sense of freedom you never had before. Without worrying about what other people think about you, you will be more productive and start living a happier life.

However, a lot of work is required to get to that point. Accepting who you are is not something that happens overnight. Each day you wake up, you must take who you are at that moment. Yet, that does not mean it is who you will always be. You must always keep growing and welcome the new you each time. Once you can do this constantly, your life will be transformed. Accepting who you are is one of the hardest things to do. Yet, when it is accomplished, your life will improve more than you ever imagined. So, stop worrying about other people's thoughts and just be concerned with what you feel about yourself. Always remember to accept yourself because who you are is pretty great.

Acceptance has meant something different at each stage of my story, and it has been a long and arduous journey. When I was younger, it was all about accepting me by having my peers understand my disability. As I grew older, it evolved into accepting my condition. Soon, it became accepting my CP not just as something I must deal with, but as part of who I am. However, at the core of it all, self-acceptance has always been learning about who I am and being okay with that answer. When you get down to it, that is one of the most critical aspects of your life: accepting yourself for who you are and being your own person.

I said it once, and I will repeat it. There is, and there will only ever be, one you. Trust me when I say that one of the best ways to waste your life is to pretend to be something you are not. Who you are is more than just good enough; you are spectacular.

It has taken me too much time to learn the importance of showing the world who I am. When you can stand alone and be proud of who you are, your life will truly begin. Continue to grow as a person, no matter what anybody else thinks. Who you are is the essence of what makes you so unique; you must never forget that. Remember that you are already more than you could ever have dreamed. Remember that you must accept who you are and become someone you can be proud of before you can unlock your full potential. But above all else, remember that who you are is pretty amazing.

7 STEPPING INTO THE RING

Stepping off the plane in New York was like stepping into a brand-new world. I felt like a kid in a candy shop; there was something new and exciting to see everywhere I looked. The sights and sounds were almost too much for me to handle. If I thought the airport was a world of its own, the hustle and bustle of New York City. was entirely something else. There was always something happening. It felt like I was an outside observer of a fantastic world I never knew existed.

Just watching it was making me tired; I felt a little worm of doubt start to set in. Was I ready for this challenge, and did I overestimate my abilities? Immediately, I put the thought out of my mind. I knew that the second I started doubting myself, everything would go downhill. I figured I was just tired from the flight, and that was why everything seemed so overwhelming. I knew that with some food and a good night's sleep, things would look better in the morning.

With that comforting thought, I knew I would overcome this new challenge before me. That night, my father and I stayed with a family friend because I could not move into the dorm yet. I tried to get some sleep so I would be ready to move in the next day. However, I found it difficult to settle down, and sleep was elusive. Whenever I closed my eyes, the worm of doubt would reappear. Eventually, I did fall asleep, but the next morning, I woke up more tired than I had been the day before.

As we drove up and saw the dorm building for the first time, I was surprised to feel a catch in my throat. I had finally made it. College life was no longer some far-off dream; it was real and starting now. The life I had chased for so long was finally mine. The first item of business was getting my school ID. I was directed to the correct building, and proudly stood for my picture. The photographer handed me my badge, and I felt like I was receiving an award.

I left with my prize firmly in my hand. I entered the next building, which would now be my home, and a security guard helped me find my dorm room. At the door, I stopped; I wanted to take a moment and drink in what this really meant. After years of pain and hardship, I had won. I was here, about to open the door to my future. From the threshold of my single room, I gazed upon my castle.

A short hallway led into the room from the doorway; on one side was the door leading to the bathroom and shower, and on the other was a decent-sized closet. As I walked further in, I saw a dresser and a desk against one wall; opposite the desk was the bed. On the back wall, there was a big window. The last thing I noticed was in the middle of the room: the recliner I had bought to help with my back pain. It had been shipped to the school a week before, and the head of the dorm office was kind enough to assemble it and put it here. I looked over my room and could not have been happier. It felt like I was one step closer to my independence. Living in a single would allow me to set up my dorm room however I wanted. This was my own little world and I could do with it as I pleased.

With help from my father and my brother, who lived in New York, I began moving in. Slowly but surely, my room started to take shape. When we were done, I took a step back to look at the room as a whole. I had put a mini fridge right beside my dresser. One of my suitcases was now at the head of the bed, doubling as my nightstand. My bathroom was set up exactly how I wanted it—posters were hanging, bringing some life into the once-barren walls, and all my school supplies were on the desk waiting to be used. With the unpacking finished, I looked around and just smiled. This was now my domain; it felt like I had built a home.

At this point, my father had to catch his flight back home. When I realized he would be leaving soon, I felt overwhelmed again. However, I pulled myself together and said goodbye. My brother had to return to his apartment, and I was alone for the first time in New York. I sat down and cried; the funny thing, though, is I had no idea why I was crying. I had wanted this for the longest time, and now that I had it, I wept. I thought to myself that maybe I needed some food. That night was the start of orientation, which began with a welcome dinner, so I cleaned myself up and went downstairs.

Walking into the cafeteria, I looked around and did not know what to do with myself. It was quickly apparent that I was younger than the other first-year students. I had just come straight out of high school and was only eighteen. But many students had taken one or two years off before college. It also became clear that most of my fellow first-year students already knew each other. However, I let none of this discourage me. My condition had caused me to miss out on a great social life, and I was determined not to let that happen again. After recovering from the initial shock of these realizations, I jumped in and started introducing myself to some other first-year students. Even though I felt overwhelmed, I knew I would need to push myself and get comfortable with my new environment.

The next day, orientation started in earnest. Each first-year student received a schedule with a list of classes taking place within the following two days—courses on navigating the campus and learning how the school's website works, a safety class, and more. I did not know I could choose which talks to attend, so I just went to all of them. By the end of that first day, I was overwhelmed and stressed by everything I heard from the classes. I talked with one of the resident advisers about my feelings. He suggested I discuss all my concerns with a member of the school's staff with whom I had started to build a relationship. I thought this was an excellent idea.

The next day, I talked with the head of the RAs and told him how I had been feeling. To my horror, I did something I had promised myself I would never do in front of anyone: I began to cry. After I calmed down, he told me two things. The first was how impressed he was that I came out to New York and how difficult it can be. He told me to forget the classes for the second day of orientation and give myself a chance to breathe. He told me I should familiarize myself with the campus and the surrounding areas. So, the whole second day, that is what I did. I walked up and down the city blocks that contained the school and everything around it. Right across the street from the campus were two restaurants I could eat at and a grocery store where I could buy anything I needed for my dorm. Farther down, there was another restaurant and a general store.

After exploring the area, I went to my dorm a made myself a shopping list. Going around to the different stores and shopping for myself was such a new and exciting adventure. I entered a drugstore and went up and down the aisles with a smile on my face. In addition to living by myself, I was able to provide for myself as well. Walking back to the dorm with the purchases in my hand, I felt nothing but pride.

As I got more comfortable navigating the campus and surrounding area, I started to feel more confident that I would succeed in New York and at school, and that more successes would follow. I returned to my dorm feeling good about myself and this new chapter of my life. I fell asleep that night with a smile on my face. I looked forward to my classes starting, but was more excited about the orientation weekend. I knew it would be a great time to further increase my comfort level with the campus, and more importantly, it would be an excellent way for me to meet new people and start getting to know my fellow first-year students better.

As I drifted off to sleep, my last thought was that my dream could be a reality after many hard years; I would get the college experience I always wanted. I would finally be free and have independence, something I had desired for so long. A dream that was for other people but never for me, it was finally mine. My CP would not get in my way, and nothing would stop me from jumping headfirst into this new adventure.

8 IT ALL HAPPENS FOR A REASON

I am six years old, and about to enter first grade. I am so excited to start school, make friends, and not feel so isolated all the time.

I had already been through two surgeries and felt like I did not belong anywhere. I just felt like the odd one out. I had no friends and felt lonely. However, in school, I could just be another kid. I could make friends and live an everyday life. The idea of being normal was so enticing to me. For too long, even into my teenage years, I held on to the idea of being average, but that's a story for another time.

Because I was six, I do not know exactly how everything happened, but I have a pretty good idea. From what I have been told, every school my parents took me to rejected me for one reason or another. One of the schools said that because of my disability, I could only attend if I had an aide with me full time. This was unnecessary; I was more than capable without help, so the school would not be a good landing spot for me. School after school was just not a good fit. Was the right one ever going to come along? Was I never meant to get the normalcy that I so desired?

Then, my parents looked at a school that finally seemed promising for me. Even before my parents explained what accommodations I would need, the principal said that they wanted me. Whatever I needed, they would give me. Without hesitation, they were ready to welcome me as a student. This was the school my parents decided to send me to. I was overjoyed when I heard the news. I was not only going to feel like a normal kid for once, but I was also going to a place where people wanted me no matter what. I was finally going to have the experiences I wanted. Unbeknownst to me, I was about to get a lot more than that. I was going to a place I could call home for twelve years.

This was the school I attended from elementary school to high school graduation—twelve years of forging relationships that I still have. Years of experience I would never trade for anything. This was the place where I grew from a child to a teenager and finally into a man. There, for the first time, I did not feel like just a child with special needs. I was a kid, no more, no less. To have that normalcy was something I never took for granted. When my life got complicated, no matter what, the school was always somewhere I could go to feel not so out of place. I would not be the person I am today without my school. That was the whole point; it was *my* school. A place that was mine. Many things were out of my control, even from a young age. So, finding a place I could call my own was significant.

It took me a long time to realize something remarkable. I started to understand that everything happens for a reason. I only went to my school because every other one rejected me. Who knows how I would have turned out if I had gone somewhere else? Everything lined up so that this was the school I was meant to go to. It was only because I found a second home that I made the relationships I have today. Every other school rejected me so I could go to *my* school. Obviously, I did not know this at the time. However, now I know many doors had to close on me so the right one would open. I was in a place where I could shut out the world around me and just be a normal kid.

IT ALL HAPPENS FOR A REASON | 65

Not to sound too cliché, but I believe everything happens in your life for a reason. The annoying part comes when you cannot find that reason. This is especially clear to me when I think about my disability. When I look back and see the hell I have gone through, the question of why always comes to my mind. Why do I have this disability? I must believe there is a reason I have my condition; if I didn't believe that, I don't think I would be able to keep fighting for what I want.

I look at it this way. I may not know why I have CP, but I need to believe I was diagnosed with it for a reason. Whatever that reason may be, only time will tell, so instead of making myself crazy with questions of why, I focus on what I can do with what has been given to me. The cards you are dealt in life might not be the best. So, rather than asking why you got the cards you did, you must play your hand to the best of your ability and know they were given to you for a reason.

Life can and will be messy; it sometimes feels like there is no rhyme or reason. One undeniable fact is that you will never know what your future holds. I have learned that sometimes you must relinquish control and trust that events in your life will take you down the best road to success. Now, I am not saying that you should do nothing, be a bystander in your life, and trust that you will end up in the right place. On the contrary, you must do your best to thrive in each situation that comes your way. Life is unpredictable. Anything and everything can get thrown at you, and it is pointless to try to determine why these things are happening to you. Instead, you must do your best and trust that all of it will make sense to you down the road.

Trusting in your efforts becomes a hell of a lot harder when you have bad times in your life. When those times happen, it can be hard to stomach that they are happening to you for a reason. When the shit hits the fan, and you feel like your whole life is in ruin, how can you be expected to know there is a reason behind this unimaginable pain? It was never easy for me to see a reason for anything when I was deep in it. Unfortunately, the only thing to do during these times is grit your teeth and fight your way out. It can be challenging, but hard times have a reason.

This lesson is especially clear to me when I look at all the surgeries I have had to go through. Trust me, as each one was happening, I was not all philosophical and saying I was going through this pain for a reason. No, in the moment, I was hurting and angry at everything. Looking back, I know my surgeries pushed me to where I needed to be. This taught me that there is always more at play than you think. Always remember that what you see is only a tiny fraction of what is happening. There are always forces you can't see working behind the scenes.

I like to think that two things happen each time you overcome hardship. The first is that you get past the obstacle and put it in your rearview mirror. This is an excellent feeling; it means you are better than whatever tried to stop you in your tracks. The second thing that happens is you get stronger. With each hardship you overcome, you gain new mental and physical experiences. With these new tools, you can be more prepared for the challenges that follow.

That is the reason for hardships in your life. Bad things do not just happen for just the sake of giving you a hard time; they come to prepare you for the really crappy moments. I think everything in life has a way of building on itself. That way, you always have the best chance when you come up against the next challenge. That is not to say bad times will hurt any less. They will still be as sucky as ever. However, looking at hardships through the lens of making you stronger might make them easier to stomach, because you know they are happening for a reason.

One of the easiest ways to understand that everything happens for a reason is to look at the bigger picture. Now, this is a lot to ask because you will seldom have the benefit of seeing how events in your life will play out and affect things as a whole. It is tough to have blind trust that you are moving in the right direction. Honestly, there is little I can do to prove my idea because it comes down to believing that you are doing the right thing. Many doors will close on you in your life. However, never get discouraged; all that means is that the right one has yet to open up. Unfortunately, you can never know when that will happen; you must trust that eventually, it will. I know this is hard. Yet, it all comes from knowing that everything in your life builds you into the best version of yourself. You grow with each new experience, good or bad, which is never wrong.

That is what it all comes down to: growth. Life is unpredictable. You can never truly know what will happen next. But I can promise that every situation you face is in your best interest; you just might not be able to see it. I know none of what I just said is uplifting, because I am saying that you do not have control over what happens in your life. However, you do have control over how you handle what is in your life. Even if it is sometimes hard to see, there is a reason for everything that happens. I hope you can let go of your uncertainty and believe that life is putting you exactly where you need to be, so you can grow into the best version of yourself.

9 JUST BE HAPPY

I have graduated from high school a few months prior, and some school friends have invited me to go to a baseball game with them.

At this point in my life, I was dealing with pain from my ankle anytime I walked anywhere. I needed surgery to alleviate it, but until then, I was not doing much because everything was too painful. I was torn; on the one hand, I wanted to go. I had not seen my friends in a long time, and it would be great to catch up. But on the other hand, I knew an outing to the ballpark would be horrible on my ankle. As I was trying to decide, a thought came to me. Pain is something I will deal with all my life, and I cannot let it dictate how I want to live. With that in mind, I told my friends I would go with them.

I was nervous on the day of the game. I knew I would be in pain, but the question was how much. Many times throughout the day, I considered telling them I had changed my mind. I kept reminding myself that I was the one who lived my life, not my pain. In the end, I stayed with my decision and told myself I would push through whatever pain I would have.

As we walked to our seats at the game, sure enough, my ankle was hurting. I thought I would have a horrible time, but I was very wrong. It was one of the best baseball games I ever went to. I had so much fun with my friends and am thrilled I decided to go. To this day, I don't remember the game's score or even the teams that played, but I do remember catching up with old friends and having a great time with them. After the game, a thought came to me. If I had let my ankle stop me from going, I would have been robbed of an experience I now cherish. If I had given in to my pain, I would have missed out on a great time and a chance to be happy.

I am in twelfth grade. I am in my school's gym shooting a basketball by myself when a classmate comes in and asks if he can join me.

I always hated when other people would join me because I was never as good as they were, and I never felt comfortable. I felt like it was just another way my CP was evident. But I was not going to be rude, so I said of course. At first, we were each just taking shots, and actually, I was making more than I was missing. I was starting to relax and have some fun.

My friend asked if I wanted to play some one-on-one. Again, I did not want my condition to show the difference between me and him, but something told me to say yes. I did, and we started playing. At least for me, the divide between our skills was becoming apparent. However, I realized I was happy and having fun instead of feeling bad about myself like I usually did. I focused on my happiness and let go of all my worries about my condition. As soon as I did, it was the best thing—we both had fun. I still smile when I think back on that day. Looking back, playing basketball with my friend taught me something crucial. When you let down your guard and worries, you open yourself up to great times and chances to be happy, which is never wrong.

Both occasions taught me something important about my life. I do and will always have some limitations.

However, I can never let that stop me from having a life. Trust me, if I kept myself from enjoying myself every time an issue with my disability came up, I would not have much of a life. Unfortunately, for a while I did live like that. For many years, I let my life be dictated by the limitations of my disability. That only brought me tears and regret. After playing basketball with my friend and going to the game, I realized that in both instances, I let go of what I thought my limitations were, and I was able to be happy and enjoy the moment.

Life is meant to be enjoyed, but sadly, people don't always follow that advice. I, for one, have spent too much time wallowing in pity and self-doubt instead of being happy. I am willing to bet that, at times, you have too. It is a very human thing to do, to only look at sadness and forget to see the joy right before you. I know I sometimes prioritize almost everything else over my happiness, but in the long run, it has never worked for me. Whenever I do this, all I end up with is a hollow feeling in my stomach.

Especially as a high schooler, I always shelved my happiness, saying it was not for me or that I would be happy in the future. However, while I was waiting for the future, I missed out on the happiness I could have had in the present. It is so easy to get distracted and lose the chance to be truly happy. But to live genuinely, happiness is a must. Unfortunately, many people look for happiness and feel like they can't find it. It's like it is always just around the corner, yet never seen. The question becomes, how can one slow down and be happy in a world full of distractions?

Happiness can be found everywhere; sometimes you have to find it, and sometimes it finds you. Joy is one of the best things humans can experience; life is not worth it unless you are happy. I cannot understate just how much happiness can impact your life. Joy is one of the most important aspects of life; without it, existence is bleak and colorless. The world is never in short supply of happiness; it is your job to find everything that brings you joy.

If you will pardon me for repeating myself, but I feel it needs to be said again. Never take the feeling for granted. Without this intense emotion, your life can pass right before you, but you will never have lived. Take it from someone who has wasted too much time—worrying and forgetting to be happy, it is never worth it. In high school, I was always concerned with one thing or another, and I cannot tell you how much I wish I could get that time back and be happy instead. Don't live with regrets. Never put happiness on a shelf for later.

There are always going to be reasons to postpone happiness. There will always be something to hold you back. Take it from me: I have held myself back because of my situation and lost out on many happy moments. You never want to live a life with regrets. I promise you that whenever you put other things above your joy, you will regret it for the rest of your life. Do the opposite of what I have done many times: Say yes to fun times and never put your happiness low on the list of priorities. Sometimes, you need to say what the hell and just go for it.

There will be a million reasons not to be happy; you need to find the one reason to choose joy, and I promise it will set you free. When you decide to let go of whatever situation you are in, and, for a short time, allow yourself to be happy, it will be the best thing you can do. If you allow yourself to throw off the chains you have put on yourself and be joyous, you will start to live a better and more fulfilling life. If you are not happy, then what the hell are you doing?

I am not saying you can always be happy; far from it. Sadly, there will be times when you feel like you will never be happy ever again. Happiness will sometimes feel like a friend you lost long ago, someone you walked hand in hand with but who vanished from your life. However, you can welcome happiness even more in these times of sorrow. I think it is a true cliché that humans only appreciate something once it is no longer around. Being a hundred miles from joy makes you want to be happier.

I will tell you a secret: Happiness is not some lost friend. It was hidden for a while but it can always return to you. You can always find something to be happy about; you might have to dig through crap to find it, but you will find it. Look, times may come when it feels like your whole world is flipped upside down. But I promise you there is still joy all around.

There is always good in the world, no matter how bleak things look. I know that everything can look like it's been stripped of color. Each way you turn, you see nothing but the worst. Yet I am telling you there is still joy and laughter. You just have to find it. I'll leave you with something I said before: There is always good.

10 THERE IS ALWAYS GOOD

I am fourteen and about to have surgery number three. It had been eight years since my last operation, and I was nervous. Honestly, though, it was more than just the nerves affecting me. Without going into too many details, I had known I was going to need this surgery for about a year. For all of eighth grade, it was hanging over my head like an anvil. I was scared, and with so much time to dread it, my anxiety only grew. I believe this is where my many battles with depression truly kicked into high gear. I had gone without a surgery for eight years, and as you can imagine, it was not easy to face the fact that I would now need another one.

I was just a big ball of stress for the entire year. I walked around with a lump in my throat and was always on the verge of tears. I worried about starting high school right after surgery and being behind everyone else, and I feared the pain I would experience. Even though this would be my third operation, I remembered very little about the first two, having had them at such a young age. So, it felt like a whole new experience for me and I had little knowledge of what to expect.

However, at the top of my list of worries was how I thought my friends would see me when I returned to school.

I did not want my classmates to think I needed this surgery because I was weak, and I did not want my friends to see me as this feeble, pathetic creature. I thought they would pity me and abandon me. Obviously, this was not true, but in my mind, it was a genuine concern.

During this period, I don't think I ever felt happiness, or anything except anxiety. Other emotions held no meaning for me. I have no idea how I got through the year more or less in one piece. This was one of the worst times in my life. Most of the time, I did not know what to do with myself. I felt like I was walking around with this unbearable weight on my shoulders. I felt like I was always a second away from bursting into tears.

People tried to help me: my parents, my teachers, and my psychologist. All these people did help me to a point, yet it felt like I was in darkness and had no way back into the light. I could hear and understand their encouraging words, but they did not make any impact on me. It was as if there was no way for me to act on what was being said. This was the first time I felt like I had truly hit rock bottom. Even when I was in a room surrounded by people, I felt all alone.

However, there was one thing I was looking forward to. Close to the end of the year, my family was taking a trip to New York and Baltimore before I would have the surgery. We were going on this trip because one of my sisters had graduated from college and the other from grad school. It was the first time in a long time that we were taking a family vacation, and I was very excited. If nothing else, I thought, this would be a time to get away from all my problems, even for a little bit.

The trip was a decisive moment because I learned what I consider to be one of the most important lessons of my life. As the family trip progressed, spending time with my family made me smile more and generally feel happy. At the end of the journey, I started to think of the long road ahead of me, and I felt depressed again. Then this idea hit me: Happiness is always around, I just needed to be brave enough to look for it. All year, I had felt like I was on the edge of an abyss, but when I let go of all my fears, looked for the good around me, and spent time with my family, it felt like sunshine was hitting my face for the first time in a long time.

I am sixteen, about to have the second surgery on my hand. When I had my hand operations within ten months of each other in my eleventh-grade year, as you can imagine, I was not doing well. I was furious and not in a good place. Honestly, it felt like my whole world was falling apart around me, and there was nothing I could do about it. I had just started the year with one surgery, which was hard enough, but having to do it all again not even a year later felt like a sick joke to me. It was so defeating that I had just fought off one challenge and before I could even breathe, another one was about to run me over.

I knew there was only one thing I could do. No matter how angry I was, I would have to prepare myself and face this new battle. But that did not mean I had to like it. During these few years when I underwent a cycle of surgeries, I was forced to be stoic in the face of overwhelming odds. However, with this stoicism came a habit of shelving my happiness until a later date. As a result, I always felt like crap.

As my parents drove me to my second surgery, I was miserable. Walking into the surgery center, I felt the buzz of a text. At first, I decided not to look, because I thought nothing I would see would make me feel better or change anything. However, a voice in my head told me that it could not hurt to see who it was. Even if it was just a scam text, at least it would be a voice from a world that I felt isolated from.

So, I looked at my phone and saw that the text was from a friend at school. I do not remember what it said, but the gist was that he was thinking of me and wished me a fast and easy recovery. When I saw his message, I smiled despite myself. I felt happy and thankful that I had such a good friend. It was like a switch was flipped instantly, and I knew I could handle everything I was about to face. Even when I felt like everything was burning down around me, the text from my friend taught me something significant. Even in your darkest moments, something good will always come along and show you the way back into the light. This one text, which was maybe two sentences, kicked me in the ass and showed me that there is always good.

I am going to be blunt: Unfortunately, there is darkness in the world. There can be so much hate that you feel suffocated by it all. Sometimes, you can feel like everything good has been washed away, and all that's left is a damaged world. There have been times when all I have seen is evil, and I had no idea if anything decent was ever going to happen to me again. There have been times when it felt like I was being suffocated by the darkness in my life. However, in moments of despair, you must remember something vital. While you are dealing with so much, it can be all too easy to see only darkness and negativity. However, there is so much more around you. No matter how bleak life may seem, there is always good. There is always happiness. No matter what, it is always within reach. You can always find something to brighten your way in the darkness.

In a world that can sometimes knock the crap out of you, it can be hard to find something to cling to; trust me, I know. So, what can you hold on to? Well, for me, it is the good that I know still exists all around. At many times in my life, I needed to cling to that good like it as a lifeboat in a storm.

It can be hard to find any good when you are enveloped in darkness. What I do is find a memory—a memory that, without fail, will fill me up with joy. My memory is that text I got from my friend before the operation. It may seem small, but that text was a raft to pull me back to the world of the living. It is always the kick in the butt I need to look around and see how good life is. With this memory, I can always remember how beautiful the world can be. Any memory can work; it just needs to be something that fills you up with happiness, something that always puts a smile on your face.

So, reflect on your life and all your happy memories. Let those memories fill you up. Let them warm your entire body and restore your hopefulness. They will help remind you that hardship is not forever, and hard times will pass. With that knowledge, you can start to find the joy and laughter that had never left you; they were right at your side the entire time. In your happiest memories, you will begin transforming into someone who can keep positivity and hope alive.

The desire to be in a positive environment is innate within all of us. However, let me tell you a harsh truth. There will be times when you will be as far from a positive environment as possible. It can be hard to imagine anything positive in those times. During those moments of negativity, you must hold on to something profound in your heart. Even in the worst kind of crap you can imagine, there is still good to be found. Hard times cannot wipe out how marvelous this world is. It might sound cheesy—bad cannot erase good; however, good can erase bad. The hard times make your happy moments even more beautiful. Seeing something good surrounded by all kinds of wrong can fill you with hope and remind you that challenges are only a passing thing.

Let me use a different word than "good"; I think being hopeful is the same as seeing the good in the world. So let me ask you a favor. Make sure to be hopeful and keep the good in your heart always. The world has a way of trying to beat it out of you. However, as you take the body blows from life, look around, and you will still find decency.

The times when all you see is pain can be enough to make you go crazy. Yet, if you can stay hopeful, your eyes will be opened to all the magic everywhere, and suddenly, that pain will lessen. This is not always easy, but it is necessary.

When you remember all the positivity that still exists in the world, I promise you will be able to get through any situation. Remembering all the good in the world fills you with fire—a fire that cannot and will not be extinguished by life's hardships.

Once you know that there is always good in this world, your whole way of thinking changes. No longer will you see trying times as never-ending battles. Instead, you will look at each one as a new chance to reform a belief your belief in the goodness around you. Bad times do not last forever, and positivity remains until the end of time. So, I must remind you to always look for the good in the world and never lose the hopefulness in your heart that can remind you of how marvelous this world is.

Never give up on the decency of this world. Even in the darkest times, when you keep hold of hopefulness, you will find just how much positivity is around you. You will understand that good is never destroyed and cannot be damaged. Instead, it can endure anything, and it is right within reach when you need it the most. There is always good in this world and don't you dare forget it.

11 THE FIRST ROUND

It's a Friday night, and I am at the welcome dinner that kicks off my college orientation weekend. Determined to finally have a social life, I sat down at a table where I knew no one. But I was sure going to fix that fast. I began talking with my tablemates, and it felt refreshing. Talking with people who did not know about me, my history, or my condition was enjoyable. The dinner went well; I met new people and felt good about myself. It was a big confidence booster.

Going from someone who never liked to draw attention to myself to a person who was able to start conversations with complete strangers was something I had never thought possible. Yet, here I was, and the pride I felt was immeasurable. As the dinner progressed, I thought I felt a change in myself; I was finally becoming the person I always wanted to be. My life was finally beginning.

However, when I returned to my dorm, I started to feel a little knot in my stomach. It was like this foreboding cloud was hanging over me. But I just ignored it. I thought I was just tired and needed some sleep. I thought if I pushed this feeling down, it would just go away.

The next day, I spent the morning with many people I had met the night before. The little knot was ever present and kept growing. Over the course of the day, it became this increasing pain in my stomach. I did not know what I was feeling, but whatever it was, I just kept pushing it down and trying not to give it too much attention. After a delightful lunch with some new friends and a teacher from the school, all I wanted was to return to my dorm and be alone.

I was starting to get a catch in my throat and felt like I was about to start crying. As this feeling intensified, my desire to return to my dorm only grew. I knew it was going to happen, and I absolutely did not want to cry in front of other people. Without being too rude, I slipped away from lunch as quickly and as quietly as I could manage.

Back in the dorm room, as soon as I closed the door, I started to cry. Let me tell you, it was not like a few sniffles. No, it was one of those full-body ugly cries—not a pretty sight. I did not even know why I was doing this, and it pissed me off that I was acting this way. I mean, less than a day ago I was feeling great. Being social and talking to new people. Yet now here I was crying in a dark room like I was a child.

Then it all made sense: I was acting like a child, and I was feeling homesick. I do not know what pissed me off more, the feeling itself or the fact that all I wanted to do at that moment was push it so deep that it would never see the light of day. I felt embarrassed and sad simultaneously. In the end, I did what I would always do when I was unsure how to handle my emotions: I pushed them down and belittled myself until I was numb to my feelings. I told myself I was being stupid and should not be feeling this way.

I stayed in the room until later that night. Eventually, I got to a point where I just was so tired of how I felt that I decided to speak to the RA assigned to my floor. As I walked to his room, I told myself I would going to pull any punches, and I was going to tell him exactly what I was feeling.

He answered the door and invited me in. As I'd planned, I told him everything, including that I was homesick. He looked me straight in the eyes and told me how he felt the same way his first weekend at college, and that it was okay for me to be feeling this way. In fact, it was normal.

This instantly made me feel better. Hearing that what I was going through was expected and average took a massive weight off my chest. I started to laugh; my RA asked me why I was laughing. I told him it was so reassuring to deal with a typical problem. After years of dealing with CP-related issues, it was funny that I was now dealing with something so standard. We had a real good laugh about that. Talking with the RA helped me immensely; knowing I was going through something part of the norm and so typical was like a breath of fresh air.

On Sunday, I was excited because I was meeting up with my cousin who lived in New Jersey. The first thing he wanted to see when he arrived at the school was my dorm room. After that, we went and got some coffee and hung out. It was like a breath of fresh air to see someone from my family. We spent all day together, and it was just the rejuvenation I needed to start my first week of classes.

After my up-and-down first weekend, I was looking forward to jumping into my classes. With the start of school, I also became familiar with my new environment. Throughout this first week, I felt my independence begin to grow. The first week's highlights came from doing things myself for the first time. The first time I did my laundry was a big day. The first time I went grocery shopping, I bought soap and a sponge and did my dishes. These might seem minor things, but for me, they were independence milestones. Every time I reached one of them, my confidence grew. Getting around and settling into New York was going great, but on the other hand, my classes could have been a little better.

For some reason, I was not enjoying my lessons. I did not know why, but I had no genuine enthusiasm for them. Then, one day, I realized there were two possible reasons I was having a hard time. First, I did not understand how to take a college course. I did not realize you had to prepare for each class and understand the material beforehand. Because of this, I would be lost in each class and did not understand what was being discussed. So, right off the bat, I was already behind.

Second, none of these were classes I had chosen for myself. Sure, they were all subjects I was interested in, but I did not choose which ones to take. I had thought having someone else create my schedule would make things easier and more accessible for me; however, without even meaning to, I had given up some of the independence I had fought so hard for. To remedy this issue, I decided to drop a class and choose a different one in its place. I felt good about myself. I saw a problem and was able to fix it myself. I could feel my confidence growing every day.

However, without even realizing it, I was falling into a rut. This was my first week, but it felt like it went on for months. My days started to blend, with no way to distinguish one from another. I was getting maybe one or two hours of sleep a night, I was barely eating, and whenever I ate, I always sat alone, trying to make myself unnoticeable. Forget about trying to socialize; all I wanted to do every day was return to my room where I could be alone. I was exhausted physically and emotionally at the end of each day. In hindsight, that really should have been a big red flag, but I was so obsessed with proving my independence that everything else was inconsequential.

This rut I had dug myself into started having consequences. I felt like crap, I was beyond tired, but I was not sleeping. I hid in my dorm room when I was not in classes, leaving me isolated. Yet, I ignored all these warning signs, to prove to myself and everybody around me that I could stand alone on my own two feet.

12 HOPE

I am in the tenth grade, having a tough time. Like most teenagers, I was unsure of where I fit into life, and I was concerned with what my friends thought of me. I was never sure of who I was. All these doubts were heightened because of my condition and my embarrassment about it. Due to all of this, I suffered from depression that I did not even know I had.

The funny thing is that I never even thought I was depressed. The way I figured was that teenagers are usually miserable, so I must be on track. It felt like each day blurred into the others, and none of them impacted me. I was just a bystander in my own life. It was like I was taking all the punches life threw at me, and all I could do was stand there and never give back any of my own. For four long, hard years, I was just going through the motions without really having any feelings at all. Day to day I was enjoying myself, but overall, I just felt defeated.

However, I kept holding on to something special through all the blows. Some days it felt beyond reason, but I would force myself through the day just so I could get home and be alone in my room. Almost every night I would cry there alone. It was almost like a purifying cry, and then I would have the strength to face the next day.

At one point during every school year, the students would gather and spend a weekend together. It was a time to get to know schoolmates regardless of which grade they were in, but most importantly, it was a time to have fun. Games were played, meals were eaten, and songs were sung. It was a highlight of every year for me. In fact, this weekend always made me feel like I was not so alone. It made me feel like I was part of a crowd instead of always standing out.

For one of the weekend activities, we would write notes to friends or whomever we wanted to. These notes were friendly little ways to tell people how much their friendship meant—a way to connect with other students in the school. In my constant misery, I would have the same thought every year that I would not receive a single note. But to my surprise, every year I would get a nice stack of letters from my friends and peers.

When I would receive these notes, it was as if I could find a little extra in the tank to keep pushing myself forward. It always meant the world to me that I had people in my life who thought I was worth the time. I was so miserable that I never thought highly of myself. So, to realize that I had people in my life who believed that much of me was one of the best feelings in the world. The notes reminded me that my friends could see past my disability, even when I could not.

I want to convey to you just a little of what I felt when I read them. So, humor me just for a second and imagine what I am saying. You are back in high school, and you are beyond miserable. Each day feels like endless reminders of how damaged you feel. You are living in consent sadness and pain, but you feel the need to plaster on a smile and pretend like nothing's bothering you. Because if for even one second you let the facade come down, you know two things will happen. The first is you will never be able to continue moving, if you let everyone see how miserable you are it is as good as admitting defeat. Second, if you let your friends see how unhappy and beaten down you feel, you think they will leave you in the dirt where you belong and look down on you with pity in their eyes.

That is how I felt every day for four years. Now, imagine that these same friends, instead of looking down on you, write letters saying how meaningful your friendship is to them and how much they enjoy spending time with you. In my hands was written proof that I was not just a waste of space and that I had friends who cared about me. I mean, there was nothing more hopeful in my life than that. It made me feel like I was doing something right.

I know I felt something, but I did not know what to call the feeling I got from reading my notes. Only later in my life could I put a name to it. Looking back, I know that this emotion was hope. Knowing that I always had friends in my corner who thought I was more than just my disability, who felt that I was a person they wanted around in their lives, filled me with hope. It gave me the strength I needed to keep pushing on even when I did not want to.

To this day, I still have all their notes, and when I feel like the world has its hands around my throat and all I want to do is give up, I pull them out and reread them. Every time, this reignites the hope I need to keep moving forward. The idea that people in my life were able to see past my disability when even I could not is something extraordinary, and I never take it for granted. If they can do that, then maybe there is hope for me to do the same.

I am in twelfth grade, having my last Color War. The Color War was an event we did at my school every year. The school would divide into two teams and we would spend a week competing in different challenges. It was one of the most highly anticipated weeks of the year. For me, it also came with worries, as you can imagine. Some of the challenges were harder for me than others, and some I had to sit out of altogether. Regardless, my schoolmates always tried to include me, and I had a lot of fun.

One event that I would never participate in was a footrace around the school. I could not run very fast, and many people would also be running around me, so I was nervous I would get jostled and knocked down. It always seemed safer to sit it out and cheer on my team. So, that is what I did every year until my last year.

As the race was about to start, I took my customary place on the sideline, ready to cheer people on. But then, I felt a tap on my shoulder. I turned around, and I saw five of my friends. One of them looked at me and asked, "Would you like to join in on the race this year?"

"It would be fun, but how would I do that?" I responded.

"With the help of us five. We all agreed we would carry you around the school so you could be part of the race."

I couldn't believe what I was hearing. It was one of the most generous offers I had ever received. I accepted with a massive smile. As they were carrying me around the school, I felt hopeful. I do not know why. It just felt like, at that moment, all was good with the world, and I could be optimistic about my future.

Later, I realized that my friends' unique act had erased some of the pain I had felt over the years. With that pain washed away, hope could shine through the cracks and fill me with life again. I realized that being there for others and showing kindness can have the most profound effect. It can bring more hope into the world. My friends taught me something I will never forget: Nothing is ever hopeless, and hope can always find a way back into your life.

Let me tell you something you already know: Sometimes, you will be pushed to your limits and even beyond. There will be times when you feel like your life has been crushed to smithereens right before your eyes. All you will want to do is sit down and cry. Trust me, I know; I have been down on the ground many times, when all I wanted to do was curl up into a ball and stay there. At times like that, it can be hard to have faith that things will ever be good again.

So, what can you do in those times? I think it is necessary to find something, anything, to hold on to that will allow you to make it to the other side. I firmly believe that hope can help you hang on. It can be your flotation device to reach calmer waters, but only if you can keep it alive in your heart.

I know it might sound cliché, but you should never underestimate the power of hope. With hope by your side, nothing is impossible. People talk about hope so much that it can lose significance. Yet, all clichés come into being because they have truth to them. The truth is that hope is the essence of what makes you human; without hope, you can never truly have any kind of meaningful life. There is no way in hell I would still be standing here today if I had not held on to hope.

However, do not just take my words at face value. Let me give you my perspective. Let me ask two crucial questions: Why is hope so important? And at its core, what is hope? Even though I ask these questions, the funny part is that I cannot answer them. Hope has a different definition for everyone.

But let me give you a description of what I think hope is. I believe hope is a dream you have in your darkest moments. A little whisper you share with only yourself to light your way through hell. A plan for a time when you will not have to rebuild your life from ashes but can live in peace. Even when all you can see is darkness, hope is believing that there still is light in the world. Hope is what reintroduces you to the world's magnificence. Simply put, hope promises a better tomorrow and the bravery to push past the pain in the present. Hope, for me, is knowing there are better times ahead, even when everything is saying the contrary. Even when all bets are against you, you know you will emerge the victor. In one sentence, hope is unwavering bravery in the face of impossible odds.

Everything I talk about in this book is complete crap if you do not have hope. That's how important hope is. It is the core that holds everything together. Hope is what gives you the strength to continue even against all odds. Hope will never quit on you, even when you want to quit on yourself. I was often ready to throw it all in and give up. My hope made me put one foot in front of the other and keep moving. When you feel prepared to accept defeat, hope will be that feeling in your heart that will get you off the mat and reignite the fire so you can keep fighting. Hope will always be the war cry of your heart. It has no fears, and all it wants is to give you the strength to reach out for your extraordinary future.

I have known pain in my life, and I can say with certainty that I would have never made it past my pain without hope. A perfect example: I would have drowned in my pain and despair without those letters I got from my classmates and peers. But because of the hope they gave me, I found my reserves of strength to keep up the fight.

To use another term, I think hope is the same thing as emotions. Emotions are the most powerful weapon in your arsenal. With emotions, you can show the depths of your character. You can show the most incredible joys or the deepest sorrows. Your emotions can show the rest of the world who you are.

Any emotion you have is proof of your hope. Even if that emotion is pure anger, you still have hope. If you can still feel something, even if it is a crappy emotion, you still have hope. It sounds a little confusing, I know. But as long as you can hold on to your emotions, you can keep hope alive. Only someone who has given up and has no more emotion can no longer have any hope. And that is not you. If you hold on to your emotions, you can always hold on to your hope.

It is an unfortunate thing, thinking you have lost hope. Assuming you have lost hope means you feel like your emotions have abandoned you. This way of thinking can lead you to very dark places; I have been down that road, and it is not fun. Let me tell you something. Even when you are in the deepest parts of hell and you think your hope has checked out, it is still there. Hope will never leave you, no matter what. It might be buried beneath all kinds of crap. But your hope is still right at your side, telling you that you will get through this dark part of your life.

All it takes is one act of caring and kindness to remove all the pain that has covered up your hope, just as it did for me when my friends offered to carry me around the school. In that one act of kindness, hope could shine brighter and fill me with newfound strength. Once hope is free, it restores you to your best self. In essence, that's what hope is. Never underestimate the kindness you give to other people. It can be the one thing they need to push past pain and feel their hope once again. With an act of love, you can give someone back their hope, and I mean, how damn amazing is that.

Hope is the vehicle that helps you on the road of life. It is what will keep the fire of your dreams alive. Hope is probably the most important thing you can have. When you have hope, anything you want in this world is possible and within reach, because you can see a brighter future for yourself. Earlier, I said that hope and emotions are the same. Emotions are the best gift humans have. Emotions give you a way to make the world beautiful; emotions give way to the best moments of the human experience. Emotions show you who you are and who you can be. Hope does the same thing. Hope gives you the ability to show the true strength you have deep inside. So, always remember to hold on to hope because it is one of your best things. Hope makes you understand what your life is and can be. It can give you the strength to keep pushing yourself forward and guide you to a brighter and better tomorrow.

Above all else, remember that even if hope feels buried beneath all kinds of crap, all it takes is one act of love to break through, and it will spring up once again. Never underestimate what an act of kindness can mean to you and someone else. It can be like a rope for someone to hold on to and find hope within themselves once again.

Because hope has become a cliché, its true meaning has become minimized, and it can be challenging to see how meaningful it is. But I know I would not be where I am today if I did not have hope. Without letters from my peers and acts of kindness like the one I got from five friends, I would not have been able to hold on to my hope. I know it kept me pushing forward even when all I wanted to do was give up. All I can say is never stop holding on to hope because it can make all the difference in your world. Hope is one of the best tools to make dreams a reality.

13 OKAY TO FAIL

I am a baby being told I will be a failure. I do not remember this story firsthand, of course, but I have heard it many times. It's almost as if I can close my eyes and see it happening. My parents had just heard my CP diagnosis and, understandably, were having a hard time with it. Wanting their questions answered, they got the name of a specialist who would give them all the information they needed. They brought me to the appointment, and the doctor examined me.

At the end of the meeting, his report was less than inspiring. This is what he said. I would never be able to walk on my own, I would never be able to talk, I would never be able to feed myself, I would never be able to live an independent life, and I would need around-the-clock care. The doctor told my parents I would be reliant on them for everything and would never be able to do anything myself all my life. In essence, the doctor said I would never lead a successful life.

Now, thankfully, that doctor was utterly wrong. Yet, as you can imagine, being called a failure when you are just a baby does leave an impact. This doctor was the first and will most likely not be the last to look at me and think I will be a failure. It is a sad fact that with my disability, some people take one look at me and assume I will never amount to anything. It is a weight I will always have to carry. Unfortunately, I almost always need to audition to prove that I will have a fulfilling life.

However, being called a failure at such a young age has also positively affected me. If only to prove the naysayers wrong, I have always worked my ass off in whatever venture I undertake. I am not saying I have never failed; I have come up short many times. However, every time I do, I hear the doctor's words, and I know I must try again and keep trying until I triumph. This doctor taught me a lesson I will never forget: Failing is okay. Not only is it okay to fail, but it is sometimes the best thing that can happen. Look, I would not have the perspective I do without getting the shit kicked out of me many times. It took me a long time to understand that I never grew during times of success. I only ever gained knowledge in the times when I failed.

I am in fourth grade, about to go on an overnight trip with my class. I experienced one overnight the year before and did well on it. So, I felt prepared for this one. These trips were a big deal to me. It was as if they were a test to see how far I had come and how strong I had become. They felt like little bits of what the real world would be like for me. If I could succeed on these little trips, I felt I would be okay in the real world. As the date for the overnight loomed, I was nervous and, at the same time, ready to prove myself once again.

The trip would start in the morning with many different activities, such as going to a trampoline park, going on a small hike, and going to an arcade. Then it was back to the school for the night, then more fun the next day. When the day finally arrived, I was ready and tackled all the activities with enthusiasm. But as the day went on, I noticed my energy level slowly dropping. I was getting more tired with each new event. However, I ignored my exhaustion because I was focused on getting another successful overnight under my belt. Unfortunately, it all came to a head at the end of the day.

Do you know that feeling of being so tired that you cannot function anymore? The kind of utter exhaustion where you can only cry because everything else requires too much effort? Well, that was the state I was in.

When we returned to school, everything fell apart for me. I think a combination of things happened. I was exhausted, and because I was so tired, I started to feel homesick. As dinner was served, I lost my composure and started crying. At that moment, I did not know why, but it felt like it was something I had been holding in all day. Teachers and friends tried to calm me down, but I kept crying. Eventually, my parents were called to take me home.

At home, my parents helped me understand what had happened to me. Throughout the day, with its many activities, I ignored my tiredness until it became too much to handle. They helped me understand that a part of growing up with my disability was listening to what my body told me and not ignoring it when I felt overly tired. Who knows, maybe if I had listened to my body and taken breaks when needed, I could have stayed on the overnight trip, and not failed.

This was such a significant point in my life. For the first time, I realized I had limitations because of my handicap. This was difficult for me to understand at such a young age. There are no such things as limitations for a normal kid, and learning that I had such roadblocks made me realize I was not a normal kid. This was the first time I understood my life would never take a regular path. I struggled with this concept for a very long time, and sometimes I still do.

This was also the first time I could remember feeling like I had failed at something. This was a new emotion for me; I felt ashamed of myself. I mean, I was okay on the class trip the year before. What had changed? I turned this question over in my mind and could never come up with a satisfactory answer. All I knew was that I had failed and could never let that happen again.

However, failing at things will happen; there is no way around it. As I continued my life and encountered more failures, I remembered the doctor my parents took me to and what that doctor had taught me. It is okay to fail.

Failing is one of the scariest things in the world; even the word can prompt feelings of weakness and defeat. Yet, what if I told you that you cannot have everything you ever wanted until you have experienced the taste of failure? You might say that I am crazy. But life will kick your ass more times than you can count, and it will feel like you are on the ground most of the time. I am here to tell you that failing is one of the best things you can do because it is the most outstanding teacher you will ever have. Only when you are at your lowest can you gain a new understanding of who you are and what you are made of.

You might think falling short of your dream is a failure, but in failing, you embark on the most important journey of all. When you are given the opportunity to fail, listen to what it is trying to tell you. If you heed its word, you will get off the ground much stronger than before.

I like to think of failing as trying. If you have ever failed at something, it means you have attempted something. When something is worth having, you must try in order to obtain it. If you fall short of your goal, yes, it means you failed, but not in a negative way. All it means is that you must try again. No matter how many times it takes, keep failing and trying until you succeed.

Failing never means the end; it is just the end of the first attempt. I know firsthand that the things that matter the most in this world will never come to you on the first attempt. Even if it takes one hundred times, you must always get back up and try again. All it takes is one time to succeed. Fail as many times as it takes and learn from each attempt so you can reach a victory. Failing at one go-around only means learning to avoid the same mistake in your next shot.

Failure is a starting point. Instead of thinking failure is a dead end, consider it a fork in the road. When you come to this intersection, you have two options: either you can quit, or you can continue to fight for what you want. If you quit, this will only lead you to darkness, and trust me, it is hard to get out of. You will get dragged down deep and start to feel angry. That hatred will continue to grow; you will turn it on yourself when there is nowhere to place your resentment. This leads to depression, which will only cause this cycle to start again.

Please take my word for it. Many times, when I reached the crossroads, I just quit right then and there, and those have been some of the worst mistakes of my life. Every time I quit; I was left with a black hole in my stomach telling me I would never be good enough. My anger would keep growing and I would turn it on myself. When I did this, I would only get more rageful. Trust me, this path sucks.

But, if you choose the path of failure, you will not find anger; instead, you will find strength. When you take the road of failure, you will find the courage to admit your faults and the power to move past them. You will receive the tools to work on yourself and become a better you. When I admitted to myself that I had overtaxed myself on my overnight trip, I did not feel a sense of crushing defeat. Rather, I found an understanding of who I was at the time. I learned how I needed to pace myself going forward to get more enjoyment out of each activity I wanted to join in on.

Instead of falling into despair about my newfound limitations and quitting, I looked at my situation and found a way to change myself. At its core, that's what failing is. It is a chance for you to look at where you are and find new ways to change yourself for the better. When you fail, it is one of the best things for you. It allows you to analyze yourself and decide if you want to grow from this experience or stay as you are.

If you choose to stay in the same place, I promise you will keep falling short. However, if you decide to grow, you will succeed every time. You can learn more about yourself from failure than you can from success. When you fall, it's important to get back up, dust yourself off, and try again. Failure forces you to improve yourself. When you fail—and believe me, you will—never consider it a negative again. Instead, consider it an opportunity to hold up a mirror, look at who you are now, and make the changes you want for the person you want to be in the future. Always remember falling down is not failure, it is just a break before you try again.

14 NOT BROKEN

I am at the start of my eleventh-grade year. It's been just a few days since hand surgery number one.

As you probably remember, I injured myself a week before school started. I fell while holding a glass cup, which shattered in my hand, and I needed surgery to repair the damage.

I had my injury on a Sunday; the operation would be on that Friday, and school was set to start the following Tuesday. Given the situation, it was clear that I would not be in school for the first day, maybe not even the first week. However, after the first day, I did not want to miss any more school, so I pushed myself to attend the second day of classes.

I held myself to insanely high standards when it came to my education and did not want to fall behind any further. Because I was down one hand, I was going to be off balance, so I went to school in a wheelchair. When I got there, I felt good. I felt strong—I had just had surgery five days ago, yet I could return to school. I had just gone through hell, but I was strong enough to make it back. I felt powerful, like nothing could stand in my way.

Because I was in a wheelchair and only had one hand available, my classmates helped by pushing me from class to class. I started my day by going to history class and a course called Introduction to Forensic Science. I was feeling good, but then I started my third class of the day, math. Throughout the class, I noticed this weird feeling. The best way I can explain it is that everything started requiring too much effort—even the small act of holding a pencil.

The more I considered this feeling, the more I realized I was probably running out of steam and needed a break. At the end of class, I asked the classmate helping me to take me to the office. I just thought I needed a little rest, maybe half an hour, and then I would be ready to continue.

My friend wheeled me to the office and headed to his next class. I explained to the receptionist that I needed to rest for a bit, and then I would go on with my day. However, as I spoke, I felt tears streaking down my face. I did not know why I started crying, so I tried to hold it in. A few of my teachers in the office saw what was going on and asked if I was okay. The floodgates broke, and I started fully sobbing.

Two things were running through my mind. One, I could not believe I was crying in front of my teachers; this was embarrassing. Here I was, a sixteen-year-old, bawling my eyes out like a baby in front of others. Two, I felt like I was broken, one of the worst feelings in the world. I felt like a weak and pathetic thing that could not even handle a few classes. In retrospect, I was just nine days out from a significant injury and only five days post-surgery. Of course, I was feeling overtaxed; it would have been insane if I was not. If I had been smarter at the time, I would have taken the whole week to recover properly and started back the next week. But at the time, I was not thinking straight. Instead, I felt like something was wrong with me; I should have been able to handle a few classes without getting tired.

I left school after that and took the rest of the week to recuperate. Even if my hand was starting to feel better, I was not. When I finally returned to school, all I could think about was how pathetic I was. Compared to all my other surgeries, this one was minor, and still it was proving too much for me. I always prided myself on being strong and overcoming all my surgeries, and this one defeated me. That thought, above all else, was so disheartening. I felt utterly broken inside.

I am in twelfth grade. With everything I have been through over the last three-plus years, it feels like I am reaching the end of my rope.

Every year, new challenges were popping up around me, and any time I tried to stand up a little, something new would come along to beat me back into submission. It was way too much for me to handle. I felt so broken inside and just defeated. I did not know how much more I could take. I was angry all the time and did not know why, and I did not know what to do with all my anger. I was shattered into hundreds of pieces and could not find them all.

One day, my psychologist recommended I discuss everything I felt with someone besides her. She said it would be a good idea for me to share myself with someone I saw on a regular basis. I took what she said to heart. Even though I was, and still am, someone who does not express my emotions, it felt like this was something I needed to do.

I knew this was important, but for the next few days, I kept going back and forth on whether I was willing to open myself up to someone and be so vulnerable. Finally, I decided it would be worth it. So, I asked one of my favorite teachers if I could talk with him. We agreed to meet at lunch, and I told him everything I felt. I still remember saying, "I just feel broken inside, and I don't know how to fix myself. I have been to hell and back so many times, and it feels like I left part of myself back there and I will never be able to retrieve it. I feel so angry all the time and I just do not know why. It feels like I am half of who I used to be. I feel so ashamed I should be able to handle everything, yet I feel like every day I am being broken into more pieces."

After I finished, he looked at me for a couple of moments. Then he made eye contact and said, "You are not broken, and there is nothing that needs fixing. You have lost nothing and must understand the difference between feeling broken and frustrated. You are dealing with a lot of emotions right now and you are getting buried by them. What you need to learn is how to feel each one as it comes. If that means crying, then you cry. If it means screaming, then you scream. You do what you need to do, and then you start moving again."

Those words changed my entire outlook. It was from this conversation that I learned a crucial lesson: There is no such thing as being broken. I was feeling an avalanche of emotions, and I did not know what to do with them; I was overwhelmed. I needed to learn how to handle my feelings when it got too much. My teacher helped me understand that emotions demand to be felt. They cannot just be bottled up and pushed down. After, you can wipe your eyes clean, stand back up, and keep fighting.

Life is going to be hard; there is no way around it. But life is supposed to be complicated; that's what makes it worth living. That said, it can feel like the weight on your shoulders will crush you. This can all be disheartening when you are dealing with one hardship after another, and there is no end in sight.

When the weight seems too much, sometimes all you can do is fall to the ground. When your life seems like endless challenges, it may seem you are losing more battles than you are winning. As this feeling sets in, you may think something is wrong with you, like you are broken. This is the worst feeling in the world; it makes you feel damaged and worthless. Feeling broken causes you to think that nothing you do matters, because you will continue to come up short.

I have felt like this many times myself. Whenever you feel this way, remember the lesson from my teacher. You are not broken; you are just dealing with a flood of different emotions. It is okay to be angry with your situation. Your emotions demand to be felt. Do not take after my example and just bottle them up and never deal with them. You must feel them.

I have learned that it is easy to think you are broken when you are experiencing a bundle of emotions. Feeling overwhelmed with emotions is like stuffing clothing into a drawer that is already too full. The harder you struggle to cram clothes in, the more they fall out. I have made this mistake many times, feeling like something was wrong because I could not handle many emotions at once. With my teacher's help, I realized there is no such thing as being broken. Instead, you feel guilty about the emotions you feel. The guilt comes from becoming overwhelmed and just feeling tired of it all. When you get overwhelmed, you may feel ashamed that the pressure has gotten to you, and you mistake all these feelings, thinking something is wrong with you.

This is something that took me way too long to learn: It is okay to feel overwhelmed. It is okay to feel the emotions so you can let them go, let them be shown. Let me tell you from experience that holding on to your feelings is one of the most dangerous things you can do. I don't know when we all got it into our heads that we need to have it together all the time. That is complete bullshit. I promise you; no one has life all together. That is the best thing I have ever understood.

Look, life is messy, and it will throw things at you that knock you back on your heels. When that happens, don't pretend like it isn't a challenge. The second you start trying to put on a brave face, the second you push down your emotions, you have already lost. Take it from an idiot who has for too long avoided letting his emotions show.

In the simplest terms, the most human thing you can ever do is feel your feelings. If you need to cry, then cry; if you need to scream, then scream. Do whatever you need to work through every emotion. Feeling overwhelmed is more than all right because it means you are human. Feel the emotions you need to, but remember, those feelings are not a sign that you are broken. In fact, they are a sign of unfathomable strength. It takes courage to feel and work through your emotions. Showing your feelings is never wrong; the weakness comes when you are bottling them up and ignoring them. Always remember that emotions demand to be felt, and after, you can wipe your eyes clean, stand back up, and keep fighting.

15 DOWN ON THE MAT

After my first week of classes, I was going the spend the weekend with the cousin who lived in New Jersey, and my brother was also lived in New York. I was thrilled it would be good to be with family. As soon as we walked into my cousin's apartment, I felt at ease, like I could exhale for the first time in a week. Being with my family, I came back into my own and felt like myself again. It was only later, in hindsight, that I realized I only felt that way while I was with them. The rest of the time, I felt like I could not catch my breath. When I was on my own, I was always anxious, looking over my shoulder for something that was not there.

I had the best time that weekend. I felt revived, until I realized I would soon have to return to school. As soon as I had this thought, it felt like someone had gut punched me. I thought this was just a sign that I did not want to leave my cousin's apartment. Not realizing what the feeling really meant, I just ignored it.

When we were leaving, my cousin could tell something was up. He asked me if I was okay. Upon hearing this the floodgates opened, and I started crying. I told him how I was feeling and everything I had been going through. He told me he had exactly the same feeling when he started living on his own, and that all my feelings were to be expected. This made me feel better and it was easier to leave his apartment.

However, the physical pain in my stomach kept growing the closer I got to my dorm. As soon as I was back on campus, I was back in my rut. If you asked me how my second week of classes went, I would not be able to answer. When I think back to that second week, nothing comes to mind. I cannot remember a damn thing that took place. In hindsight, I think that is a testament to how unhappy I was and how depressed I had become. All I know for sure is that the stress of my classes was starting to get to me. I soon found that I was way behind and needed to catch up on my schoolwork. Whenever I would finish an assignment, five more would pop up, demanding to be done. Added to this was my minimal eating and my lack of sleep, which was maybe an hour or two a night. Very quickly I had been caught in a downward spiral.

However, there was a light at the end of the tunnel. My sister and I went to the same school, and we had a monthlong break coming up during which we would be returning home. Going home so soon after arriving in New York annoyed me a little. I felt like I had made progress in becoming accustomed to the city and getting comfortable with everything (maybe not my schoolwork, but everything else was going well). I worried I would lose the confidence I had gained if I left for a month.

But at the same time, I had a nagging thought in the back of my mind. Maybe I had held it together for the first two weeks because I knew I would be home soon. Perhaps I only felt like I was succeeding because I could expect the trip home. This thought was disheartening. Something was becoming clear to me: I could no longer ignore all the emotions I had been feeling these last two weeks. The longer I ignored them, the worse there would be when I finally let them out. I decided that the upcoming break would be a perfect time to analyze and move past them before I returned to school.

Even though I told myself I needed to work out my feelings, I continued pushing them deeper when I got home. Dealing with my emotions meant I would have to admit I had difficulty adjusting to my new life, and I was very much out of my depth. I was not ready to accept that; I was determined to prove that I could be independent. No matter what, I needed to succeed in my new life and at college. The independence that had eluded me much of my life was finally in my grasp, and there was no way I would lose it. So, I rationalized all these emotions as growing pains and getting used to my new environment and ignored them more.

But no matter how much I tried to ignore these feelings, I kept having mini breakdowns during the break. Whenever I thought about returning to school, I felt a massive weight on my chest. I lost count of how often I cried about returning to New York. However, I was still so obsessed with doing something that was not related to my condition that I continued to push these feelings deeper. The idea of admitting my feelings, even to myself, felt like a slap in the face. It would mean I had failed if I acknowledged I needed help. So, any time I felt some emotion, I would cry a little but then bottle it up fast.

Suddenly, it was time to go back to school and my new life in New York. My sister and I were taking a red-eye flight back, and leaving was much more complicated than expected. The night of the flight, all our luggage was ready in the entranceway of our house. Every emotion I had felt during the vacation hit me at once, and I started crying. I calmed down, and yet again, I pushed the emotions into even more darkness and ignored them. I knew I needed to pull myself together.

The flight was long, and finally, early in the morning, I returned to my dorm. It was a hard night, but I thought I would start feeling better once I returned to my routine. I did not realize that what I had was not a routine, but rather a rut. The second I was back in the dorm room, without knowing it, I turned back into a ghost of my former happy self. Once again, I stopped sleeping and was barely eating. Things were not looking up. I needed to catch up on my schoolwork. I constantly felt anxious, and I had no idea why. Gone was my prior confidence; it was like I was just trying to survive minute to minute and not break down and cry. Something was badly broken in me.

Two days after returning, I hit rock bottom. I got back to my dorm room after a long day. As I looked around the room, I felt disgusted. I hated this room like I had never hated anything before. I only saw a prison cell. I brought dinner back with me and ate it by myself. It was tasteless; I ended up eating less than half. Then, it was time to turn my attention to the mounting pile of homework and start doing one of the assignments.

I do not remember what the final straw was, but finally I just had enough. I was so tired, so hungry, so unbelievably defeated. I did not know what to do with myself anymore. I was a just done. I had failed myself and everyone around me; everything I had tried at, I had failed. I tried to live alone, and I felt isolated and sad. I tried to be a good student, but the mountain of unfinished assignments mocked me. I was such a failure at living independently that I could not even get myself to sleep and eat properly. I had taken body blows one after another and was down for the count. I had just gotten my ass handed to me and I no longer had the will to fight back. I was ready to throw in the towel.

I sat down on the floor and let out a scream. A scream filled with anger, pain, sadness, and just pure, unadulterated hate for no one but myself. My blood ran cold; I was no longer worthy of it circulating through my body. New York had taken its pound of flesh. I knew I could blame no one else for my situation and hated myself more. I have no idea how long I sat on the floor, but suddenly, every mistake came rushing back, and every feeling I had pushed down came at me at once. An earthquake of emotions rocked me to my core, and I felt myself falling deeper into a pit of misery. I saw the knife I had used with my dinner, picked it up, and looked at it. Knowing what I wanted and needed to do with it.

16 NEVER GIVE UP

I am in high school, and my classes are becoming a real struggle. I also have a fair amount of learning challenges in addition to my physical limitations. I have some dyslexia, trouble writing, and difficulty following along with the lessons and taking good notes simultaneously.

When added up, these factors made schooling difficult for me. With my physical disabilities on top of that, school was next to impossible. Even so, I was a solid student, with passing grades most of the time. But behind the scenes, those grades were only possible with hours of hard work. I could only keep up with the workload with help from many different people, from teachers to other students. There was no way in hell I could have done it myself. With each passing year, it became apparent that graduating from high school was no longer a question of when, but if ever.

Sometimes I felt like I was drowning in my schoolwork. I felt different from the students who could breeze through classes and their work like it was nothing. It took hours of beating information into my brain just to achieve passing grades. Despite all these challenges, and beyond all reason, I kept getting closer to graduating.

It felt like a dream when I was finally on the stage at graduation. Sitting up there, I was hit with a wave of emotion. I realized I was not graduating by mistake; it was because of hard work that I was here. I have never been a stranger to working hard and persevering. I mean, hell, that was the majority of my life with my disability. However, this was the first time I had accomplished something outside the realm of my condition. I achieved this not because my disability commanded it of me, but rather because I wanted to. Sitting up on that stage meant more than just getting a diploma. It was a shining moment of recognizing all the hard work I had done, and in that moment, I understood what it meant never to give up.

I am in my fourth-grade year. I've just learned that in PE class, students are required to run a mile. When I heard this, I was concerned for obvious reasons. My first thought was to find a way to excuse myself from this assignment. But the more I thought about it, the more I realized that if I used the CP as an excuse to get out of running this mile, I would never be able to forgive myself. If I used my disability as a "get out of jail free" card, it would be hard for me to stop, and in the long run, I knew I would just be hurting myself.

If I backed down from this, I would never stop backing down, and that is no way to live. I wanted a life of strength and courage, where nothing, not even my disability, would stop me. The more I thought about this mile, the more I realized that this was a proving ground for me. It was an opportunity to show myself that I could do anything I wanted. If I could finish this mile, I would feel like a normal kid like anyone else in my class. I thought if they could do it, so could I.

I was not oblivious; I knew accomplishing this goal would not be easy. But I was ready for the challenge. On the day of the mile, I adopted a mentality that I would finish no matter what. The test was to take place on the school's soccer field behind the building, and four laps around would be required to complete it. I looked out at the grassy field and saw my Everest. The starting line would also be the finish line. I saw the white paint outlining the soccer field and my running track.

The grass billowed in the slight breeze. I could feel my heart beating hard in my chest. I was nervous, and I could feel myself sweating. A voice in my mind told me I would not make it. I tried to ignore it and focused on the task before me. I quieted the butterflies and prepared myself for the road ahead. I calmed my breathing, steadied my mind, and became intensely focused; I was ready. I approached the starting line with the rest of my class. I looked at the gym teacher, waiting for the signal. Each second lasted an eternity. This was it; it was time to see what I was truly made of. The teacher raised her hand and told us to start.

I started running with the rest of my class. However, I quickly fell behind, and by the time I started the second lap, most of my peers had already finished. I completed the lap and was the only one left running, but I knew I would finish no matter how long it took me. I was tired by the middle of the third lap, but I kept telling myself I would complete the mile even if it killed me.

When I made this declaration, life threw a little test at me. I fell hard, face down on the grass; I admit that my conviction faltered. But I pushed myself back up and kept on running. Then I fell again. I was utterly exhausted and had no more strength; I was ready to give up. I had failed my goal. Every muscle in my body was on fire, and the thought of getting up again was torture.

I eventually pushed myself off the ground. As I got up and was about to tell the teacher I was done, I saw that the class had stayed behind to watch me finish, and they were not the only ones. Teachers and other faculty were also waiting at the finish line for me.

I found an eruption of strength and could keep going. But during the fourth and final lap, I was again ready to throw in the towel. I was beyond drained. Every muscle in my body protested for me to stop. I was prepared to listen to my body immediately. I felt like crap. I had come so close to finishing my dream, but I thought I could not take even one more step. It was demoralizing to know I had come so far, but could not make it to the finish line.

At that moment, I thought of the declaration I made to myself. I was going to finish this mile even if it killed me. Not wanting to fail, I started to walk slowly. With each step, I repeated my mantra—I will finish even if it kills me—over and over to myself. My strength was reignited; I knew I had found what I needed. Suddenly, I was able to start running again. I pushed past the pain, and the finish line started to come closer. When I crossed it, all my friends came to congratulate me. It was the best feeling in the world. When it mattered the most, I didn't give up on myself and found the strength to achieve my goal. I had the power to do anything I ever wanted to do, despite my disability (or maybe because of it), if I never gave up no matter what.

Life is made up of challenges. You win some, and you lose some. But no matter how often you find yourself on the losing side, you can never give up. Promise me that no matter how much pain you are in, how battered and bruised you might be, or how much you want to raise your white flag, you will fight tooth and nail until the final bell rings. You must commit to leaving everything you have on the field every day. No matter what comes your way or how hard things may seem, you can never quit on yourself. Sometimes, you get sucker punched by life and find yourself wondering if it's worth getting off the floor in those times, you must stand and never back down.

Anything worth having in this world will not come easy. When you have a dream, this is precisely when life will test you. When you have a goal in mind, you must never give up on it, no matter what life throws your way. When you find yourself in life's headlock, you only have two options: quit or fight.

Dreams are always an uphill battle, and you must start the climb, no matter how tall the mountain might be. Even if you fall and slide back down to the bottom, get back up and start again. It might take you one hundred attempts to get to the top. Yet, you must keep going. Keep moving forward and save a picture of your dream in mind. That mental picture will give you the durability to keep fighting. I promise you that the harder you work at something, the more beautiful the reward.

It will always be easier just to quit than to keep going. The pain will stop, and you will no longer have to deal with hardship. Pretty enticing, I know. Yet, I promise, if you quit, you will regret it for the rest of your life. Because you are not just quitting on whatever challenge is in front of you; you are giving up on yourself, which is inexcusable. To quit on yourself is one of the worst things you can do. Throwing up that white flag is telling the world and yourself that you are not strong enough to go after what you want.

Let me tell you from experience: If you decide to give up, you will never forgive yourself. The second you make that decision, the only person you will have to answer to is yourself. In times when I chose to give up, it always felt like the best option in the moment. However, something would always start gnawing inside me. Regret would grow until it was almost too much to handle. Your shame will feel worse than anything life can throw at you.

However, when you decide not to give up, not to let the pain and hardship defeat you, something unique will happen. Many new doors will open for you, and you will realize that nothing is impossible. You can do whatever you want in this world, but you must be willing to take what life throws at you and throw it right back.

If you feel like giving up, I want you to do something. Close your eyes and look deep within yourself. Then, ask yourself, are you prepared to give up on your dream? The answer must always be no. Even if answering yes seems like the best option, always answer no. Every time you respond with no, you will keep fortifying your resolve. That resolve will make it that much harder for you to give up. Whatever happens to you, you must always answer no. Always keep pushing for your dreams.

Life itself is meant to challenge you, to push you to become the best version of yourself. With every obstacle, you become that much stronger. Never shy away from a challenge and quit on yourself. Challenges are not given to stop you in your tracks; challenges are designed to help you grow and to guide you to achieve your dream. In its simplest terms, not giving up means to keep moving. You must always find a way to push yourself forward. You must continue toward your goal by running, walking, crawling—whatever it takes—as long as you keep moving. When you find something blocking your path, it is a chance for you to prove your courage, draw from past obstacles, and use your newfound durability to overcome hardship.

I want you to do something right now. Put your hand on you chest, quiet your mind, and listen to your heartbeat, the rhythm of it beating against your chest. The rise and fall of your chest, the sound of your breath. Do you know what that sound signifies? That you are alive, and you are still moving forward. It means that past events did not stop you; you never quit in the past, so why would you give up now? If you ever feel like giving up, all you need to do is look back on your life and see how far you have come. While you are still alive, there is no reason to give up. With each heartbeat, you must fight for what you want and always give everything you have.

Let me paint you a picture. Imagine having a dream, something you have wanted your whole life. Everything you have done has been to achieve your goal—nothing else in the world matters but making your dream a reality. But then, an obstacle comes your way, and you will never be able to reach your vision until you move past it. No matter how often you try, you keep falling short of this challenge. You start to feel discouraged; you keep fighting but cannot get over the finish line. As disappointment sets in, you want to give up and stop trying.

At this point, you have reached a crucial crossroads. You can either give up or continue to fight for your dream. If you decide to give up, imagine how you will feel. You will hate yourself. All your self-doubt and all your fear will come crashing down around you, and you will never want to try for anything again.

Trust me; it can be a crushing feeling. The other option is to keep trying no matter what. No matter how many times you fall, you keep pushing yourself off the ground and trying again. Even if you fall one hundred times, it is that 101st time that allows you to finally move past the obstacle. Once you achieve your goal, you will feel like you climbed your own Everest. You were brave enough to tell yourself it is okay to fall many times; you just needed one time to work. The feeling you have will be intensified because you know that you never let anything stand in your way; you kept on pushing and moving forward. You can smile because when you were faced with the option of giving up, you made the right choice and kept getting off the floor.

Challenges will come into your life. Some will be easy to overcome, but other obstacles will seem nearly impossible to pass. Never let this beat you down. There is always a way to overcome any obstacle, even if it is not apparent. But if you give up when you cannot pass a challenge, you do a great disservice to yourself. You tell yourself and the world that you are not strong enough to achieve your dreams. If you decide to fight instead of quitting, I promise it will be your best decision.

You can never quit because, unfortunately, if you do it just once, it will become a habit. Instead of facing anything hard, you will give up because it is easier. But quitting can never be an option for you. The only way to prevent hardships from stopping you in your tracks is to keep going; the only way to stop a difficulty is to fight through it to the other side. To obtain whatever you want for yourself, you must be willing to take whatever comes your way. You must be prepared to go through hell. But if you can get to the other side, I promise it will be more than worth your while. Going into combat for what you want will be challenging, but claiming victory will be all the more precious.

You must find out what kind of difference you can make. When you decide to fight, to keep pushing yourself forward rather than giving up, you can also inspire others around you not to give up on themselves, which is powerful. You never know who is going to see the strength you have and find that strength within themselves. That is the true power of never giving up—it benefits you and can also help the people around you.

You can be someone's reason to keep trying, and because of you, they can then be a reason for someone else not to quit. Your decision can affect so many other people's lives in unimaginable ways. You can be such a positive presence in this world, and all that starts with your refusal to give up. So, let me put it this way: If you ever feel like quitting, even if you do not want to continue fighting for your sake, keep pushing yourself for those you care about. Speaking from the heart, there have been many times I wanted to give up and did not care what happened to me. But knowing I could be an inspiration for others would, without fail, give me the courage to get back up and keep fighting.

There will be times in your life that will push you to the limit. I had many times when I wanted to give it all up. When I just wanted to shut the whole world out and never try for anything ever again. One thought always comes to me when I am in a dark place. Being in a state like that is no way to live. You cannot live your life in the shadows, no matter how much you may want to. Whenever I had this thought, I knew I had to keep trying and living my life. Trying times will come, but only you can decide if they help you grow or help destroy you. Look, there is only one way to live life—fighting for dreams—and the only way to do that is to never give up on yourself, no matter what.

Life can be difficult sometimes; it can be messy and unpredictable. But that is the true beauty of life; it pushes you and challenges you to be the best you can be. To never give up is to say to yourself that no matter what comes your way, you will face it head-on and overcome it no matter the odds. To keep pushing on when you think you cannot, is what makes all the difference in your life.

So, never raise that white flag, no matter how many times you fall or how much pain you are in. Never give up on your life; let your past experiences and relationships wash over you and give you the courage to keep fighting. You have so much more in you, so get off the ground, dust yourself off, keep fighting for what you want, and always remember: Never give up.

17 YOU CAN ALWAYS CHANGE

I am in ninth grade, and not starting my high school career as I thought I would. I am coming off my first surgery in seven years, trying to navigate my recovery and the assignments that keep piling up.

Thankfully, during this time in my life, my teachers and physical therapist understood and let me do things at the pace I needed. Regardless of the support I was receiving, it was a tricky juggling act. As my rehab and workload ramped up, I quickly felt like I was losing balance. My life was dominated by either physical therapy or schoolwork.

As I tried to push through each challenge, one thought kept coming to mind: I wished I could travel back a year to when I was not dealing with any of these issues. A fantasy of living in the past when times were more straightforward was tempting. Obviously, it was impossible, but it was still nice to think about it, like a silent wish I knew would never happen. Regardless of my impossible desire (or maybe because of it), I learned a hard reality of life.

Something hit me as I looked at my yearbook at the end of the year. While I was so consumed with the idea of living in the past, I missed all that was happening around me in the present. I realized I had finished my rehab and caught up on all my work a few months into the school year. Most of my stress should have been gone, yet I still spent the rest of the year wanting to live in the past. While I tried to live in a fantasy, I missed out on good times in the present.

At that moment, I understood that something needed to change. A circumstance like the one I experienced at the beginning of the year would inevitably recur, and I was determined to avoid making the same mistakes again. I decided to look at the past year as a guideline. I had looked at the beginning of the year as a challenge rather than an opportunity to learn how to balance aspects of my life. Upon realizing this, I stumbled upon another lesson: Change is a requirement for life. No matter how much I had wanted to live in the past, I needed to adapt to my new reality. I had to change my perception of my life and start growing into a new me.

I am in eleventh grade, taking a trip with my classmates to Washington, DC. I cannot pinpoint exactly when this happened, but during the trip, I realized I did not want to be just part of the crowd anymore; I wanted to be my own person. I wanted more for myself. I did not want to blend into a group; I wanted to stand out and be more than just a follower. Maybe it was because I would start college in two years, or perhaps it was something else. But I knew it was time to grow and evolve into something new.

I returned from the trip and sensed that the time of growth was upon me. To start this process, I needed to ask myself what was more important, acting one way to be accepted, or becoming someone I could be proud of and not caring about what other people thought of me. I knew this would require some profound changes on my part. I was petrified of changing, but I knew I needed to if I wanted to become the new me. My mind was made up the week after the DC trip; it was time to change and evolve into my own man.

I recognized that this challenge would make me stand out. I hated standing out for any reason. I already looked like the odd one out with my crutches, and now I wanted to make myself stand out more. Was I crazy or something? I figured, yes, changing might make me stand out more than I already do. However, to grow, I knew I needed to become someone I could be proud of.

This was scary for several reasons. I was unsure if my classmates would accept the new me, and I did not know what I wanted the new me to look like. So, I had to sit down and think about a few things. The first thing I did was make a couple of lists. On the first list, I had to be honest about myself, and I wrote down everything I wanted to change and everything I disliked about who I was as a person. On another list, I wrote how I wanted to see myself. I wrote down what I wanted out of my life and how I would achieve my goals. These lists were difficult to make, yet they were an essential step. I understood that the only way to make lasting changes was to be brutally honest and nitpick everything about me. It was almost like I had to destroy myself before I could build myself up again.

I looked at all the lists and matched them up. I matched who I was now to who I wanted to be; then, I checked whether I could reach my goals with the changes I wanted to make. Now that I knew how I wanted to grow, I returned to my first concern: how my classmates would react to my changes. Something hit me as I considered this. Why should I give a crap what my classmates, or anybody for that matter, thought about me?

It was so crystal clear all at once. What my classmates think about me (or what anybody thinks, for that matter) should never affect how I feel and what I think about myself. Why should my peers' opinions affect whether I liked the changes I made for myself? The way I saw it, if my friends didn't like the new me, they might not be the right people to hang out with. I understood that the friends who accepted the new me were my true friends.

After this realization, I made the changes I wanted to. I started dressing nicer, talking more maturely, growing up, and showing that I was ready to be an adult and move forward. I began to stand out as my own person. I was nervous the first day I came to school as the new me, but I told myself I needed to stick with the changes I had made. Because I knew in my heart, I had made the right decision.

Over the next couple of days, I was shocked. Instead of looking down on me for the changes, people regarded me with newfound respect. Some even approached me to compliment the changes they noticed. Many of my classmates told me I looked more confident than before. In the following weeks after my evolution, I understood something compelling. Change needs to be a certainty in life. I needed to keep growing, or I would hold myself back and live in the past.

Never let how people view you stop you from improving yourself. It should never even come into the equation. Some people might leave you high and dry when you evolve. But do not look for them; look for the people who have stayed by your side always. Your true peers are those who will never judge you but will encourage you and cheer you on when you change yourself for the better. Never underestimate the ripple effect you have on your surroundings. As you grow, you will realize that the people around you also want to change. Like you, they may be scared to take that first step. Yet, when they see that you did it and bettered yourself, it will inspire them to do the same.

You can be the catalyst that changes yourself and the people around you. I firmly believe that you will have the same experience I did. When you realize it is time to change something about yourself, I know you will be scared and might decide it is not in your best interest. But I promise, doing it anyway will be one of your best decisions.

However, that decision comes with a stipulation: The changes you want to make must be for you, to make yourself better. They must not come from a feeling that if you change, people will like you more. When you grow, you must grow for yourself. If you change for any other reason, sooner or later, your decision will come back to bite you in the ass. You must never forget that if you like yourself and the changes you have made, it does not matter what anybody else thinks.

Life is all about evolving. Yet, change can be challenging. It's easy to feel like who you are now is who you will always be, and it can be scary to change into who you want to become. Growing into a new you takes tremendous courage, but I promise you, it will be the best thing you ever do. It is only when you take that all-important first step that you begin to appreciate just how strong you are. It means you are brave enough to look deep inside yourself and say that you understand you can be better and will do what is necessary to make it so.

Growing is vital to your life; without it, you will never reach your full potential. Just imagine how discouraging it would be to know that you left your true potential untapped just because you were afraid to change things about yourself. Now, imagine how amazing it will feel when you take that first step. There is no telling what you can accomplish. All it takes is bravery and a willingness to look at yourself and grow into a better you. A you that can change the world. A you that will achieve unbelievable things.

Be honest; you have parts of yourself that you want to change. I know I sure as hell do. It is always hard to admit that you have traits you dislike. However, you will never be able to move forward until you can be brutally honest with yourself. Once you can be forthcoming, you can begin the road to self-improvement.

So, how do you go about changing yourself? It is not an easy path to take, but it is a vital one. It will take time; growing is a process you must constantly work at. Growth must be a state of mind; it is a thought process you must always follow. Changing yourself is a declaration that says you are ready to cut away your negative traits. That you are willing to look in a mirror and see a different version of yourself in that reflection.

Change can be scary because it means saying goodbye to who you once were and taking a leap into new and unknown chapters of your life. But if you refuse to change, you are clinging to a past already gone. You cannot live in the past, no matter how much you may want to. The past is gone, and it is never coming back. When you are prepared to change, you can start living in the present and will be able to look toward a bright future.

The marvelous thing about change is that you always have a chance to do it. You can decide to grow and better yourself at any moment. You can do it right this very second. There are 1,440 minutes in a day, each a new opportunity to start a new journey. You have 1,440 opportunities a day and then another 1,440 chances the next day, and so on. With so many occasions, why would you not take one of them?

It can be scary to change and even more intimidating to take that first step into the unknown. It is worth it because once you take that step, all the steps after that will be much easier. But it all comes down to the first step. You need to be willing to say, "That was the old me, but now I want to be different, better than I think I can be, better than other people think I can be." Change might be challenging, but let me tell you, the things in life that scare you to hell are the most worth it. You can reach your highest potential when you decide to change.

Making changes is not something you do for others; it is something you do for yourself to help you grow. Changing is one of the most courageous things you can do for yourself. You know you can always be better and do better; that is what changing is all about. It's about saying that who you were in the past was good, but you know you can and should push yourself to become more impressive than before. Change yourself so you can change the world. Grow so you can inspire others. But above all else, evolve because you want to become the best version of yourself that you know you can be.

Learning to accept who you are is so important. With that being said, who you are tomorrow can be different from the person you are today. Keep growing, keep evolving. No matter what, always keep moving forward. Always remember there are 1,440 minutes in every day and 1,440 chances to become a better you. Use each one wisely and to the fullest, and always keep growing. Keep becoming the best version of yourself.

18 PAIN IN A NEW LIGHT

I am five years old, having my first surgery. My hips were coming out of my sockets, and walking was becoming increasingly difficult. Not to mention the pain I was in. Being only five, there was no way I was prepared for the pain after the operation. The surgery left me in a full-body cast that came up to my chest. I was in the hospital for about two weeks, then home for about six with the body cast. In hindsight, being unable to move was a blessing in disguise. Yes, I was in pain, but not as much as I was about to be in.

After six weeks in the cast, I returned to the hospital for the doctors to cut it open, and I was able to be out of it for short periods. I was so happy. I thought this meant my constant pain would be over, but I was wrong. The first time I got out of the cast, I felt like my legs were full of pins and needles every time I tried to take a step. My pain was worse than before; I did not even think that was possible.

After weeks without using them, my muscles had atrophied, and it was excruciating to put weight on them. This meant weeks of hard and painful therapy to regain my lost strength. I was not even gaining new strength, just returning to square one. It was demoralizing having to fight for something I once had, and it made no sense to my five-year-old mind. At that age, I thought surgery was supposed to fix me, not rip something away from me. All this surgery did was give me added pain. It all seemed so unfair. Standing, sitting, walking, and even lying down was painful. There seemed no end in sight to my misery. Yet, at the same time as I was hurting, I also learned something valuable.

Despite all my hardships, my mother would always tell me that every morning I would wake up with a smile and try my best to be happy. Even at a young age, I understood that if I did not master my pain, I would be buried by it. I decided I had two options: let the pain take hold and be miserable, or be happy and enjoy myself despite my suffering. Sadness and pain do not need to go hand in hand. Believe me; it is only too easy to let pain bury you in misery. Yet I did not let that happen. Without realizing what I was doing, I constantly tried to be the best version of myself regardless of my pain.

Physical pain should never be a roadblock to happiness. By just smiling and being happy all the time, I was telling my pain that it was not the master of me. I have held on to this idea throughout all the painful times in my life. I could rise above my wounds by showing up as the best version of myself whenever I was going through hell. Not only could I master my pain, but during my third surgery, I found that doing this had another benefit.

When I returned to school after my third surgery, I was again trying to put my best self forward and smile through my pain. My classmates knew what I had just gone through. Numerous people came up to me and said that it was inspiring to see that even though I was in pain, I still smiled and was happy. I put on a smile for others even though inside I was suffering.

After hearing many comments like this, I understood that putting my best self forward was having an unintended consequence. People saw how I was acting and drew strength from that. For me, that was pretty damn cool. It was also the first time I understood that, like it or not, just by the nature of my condition, people would watch me and see how I acted. What also blew my mind was that pain was teaching me all these lessons. With this in mind, I started looking at pain in a whole new light.

After four years of struggle, I am graduating. As you know, my high school years were challenging. Yet through all the crap I endured, I had finally reached this moment. From my many obstacles, I learned that there are two kinds of pain: physical and emotional. My past surgeries had clearly been all about managing physical pain. But high school taught me what it meant to be in emotional pain. After four harrowing years of experiencing both types of pain, I was battered and bruised, and I had some new scars as trophies.

However, I had finally made it. I was here, about to graduate. It was the proudest day of my life. It felt like I had proven all my naysayers wrong. If I am being completely honest, it is a day I never thought I would see. With everything else I had to deal with, my academics always had to take a back seat, so graduation was a significant accomplishment. Along the way, the end of high school had always felt so far from where I was, almost like it was a reality for my classmates, but not for me.

In the venue where the ceremony was being held, there was a small room for getting ready. At one point, the class was preparing to take pictures outside. I told them to go ahead and that I would catch up with them. Alone in the room, I pulled up a chair and stared at a blank wall. I was overcome with all kinds of feelings. I needed a minute to realize what this moment really meant for me.

Sitting there, I could not help but think of everything that had happened over this long journey. I looked down at the scar on my hand, where I had cut it with glass a year before. I could feel every cut on my body that those surgeries had inflicted. I felt the emotional wounds that had made me cry long into the nights. It suddenly became too much, and I thought I needed to scream. However, at the same time, I also wanted to cry tears of happiness.

As I considered everything I had been through, one thought bubbled up. I would not have changed a thing about my past. This admission surprised me; I had always wanted things to be different for as long as I could remember. However, sitting in that room about to graduate, I realized that everything I went through had gotten me to this point. All the shit I had been through, I was proud of. I would not be me if not for everything I had been through. All the physical pain and emotional torment molded me into someone I was proud of. Someone who always did the right thing no matter what. Who would always help a friend in need and put others' needs before his own.

At that moment, I understood I am the sum of my experiences, and without them, I would be someone unrecognizable. In that room, I realized how my pain had forged me. I realized that pain of any kind gives you more than just scars. Like clay, these moments of pain formed me into who I am, and I am damn proud of the person I have become.

There is a difference between the two types of pain: physical and emotional. Physical pain is the easiest to understand. You cut your finger, and it bleeds; you hurt your toe, and it turns black and blue. It is an occupational hazard that you will get hurt. If you show me a person who has never gotten any scratch, broken bone, or cut, you have just offered me a person who has never truly lived. To live a life to the fullest means you will get messy and hurt.

Nothing can be done to prevent physical pain; it will happen to you, and you must deal with it. The only thing you can control is how it affects you. The thing about physical pain is that everyone can see it. You cannot hide if your arm needs a sling or a cast. To let an injury heal, you often must put something visible on your body. The fact that people can see this pain is one of the reasons it is so powerful. I think, in a way, that visible pain can inspire people. Simply put, you can use your pain as a source of strength. You must ask yourself some essential questions when you get hurt physically: How much more pain can you take? How much are you able to endure and still have a smile on your face?

Sometimes, life will be measured by something other than the number of your achievements. At times, it comes down to how much physical pain you are in and whether it causes you to break. From my experience, the times that will matter most will be when you are battered and bruised, yet you can still smile and face each new day with hope for the future. If you can do that, I promise you can overcome any physical hardship, no matter how wounded you are.

Countless times, I was in unthinkable pain. Bruised and bleeding, but still standing. For a fact, I know my actions inspired others—people who saw how much pain I was in, yet simultaneously saw me smile and put others first. I was able to inspire them because I understood that if I let my pain control me, it was a slippery slope. I needed to wear a brave face and keep smiling to avoid wallowing in pain and self-pity. I will not lie, it was not always easy. Sometimes, I was in so much pain that it felt like I was drowning in blood. However, I would say to myself that the only way to get through hell is one step at a time, and I might as well be smiling with each step.

Imagine that you've been hurt badly, but you can still smile and be happy despite your injury. People around you will see this and think to themselves:

"Now here is a person who got badly hurt, but instead of sitting around and feeling sorry for themselves, they can still be happy and positively impact the world. Well, surely if they can act this way, even though they are in a great deal of pain, then any problems I have, I should be able to handle with the same attitude."

When you decide to be your best self, even in your worst times, the impact on the people around you is just incalculable. If you decide that come high or hell water, injury or no injury, you will be happy and positive, then other people will act similarly. When you hide your pain and put other people first, it shows just how strong you are, and your strength will inspire others to do likewise.

You never know who will see you being strong and might need that boost of motivation. You can either let pain stop you, or you can use it to inspire hope in others. No matter what shape you are in, if you can put it away in a box and be there for others in need, you will find that your agony slowly starts to dissipate. The strongest person can use their hell to inspire hope in others. I am not saying that dealing with pain is easy, but when you try to show up and, despite your pain, be happy and positive for other people—well, it shows how strong a person you are.

Now, the second type of pain is emotional pain. Let me be straightforward: This pain is much worse than the first. Nothing that physical pain can throw at you will ever be worse than your emotional scars. Emotional pain is something that you walk around with your entire life. It may lessen over time, but stays with you forever; it is your baggage. Physical scars will fade, but the wounds you get from emotional pain stay fresh always.

However, that is not a bad thing. The best way I can explain emotional pain is like this. When something so horrible happens, you feel like the only way to express your emotions is to scream, but this scream is born from something different. It is a scream made of pure anger caused by tears and fear. It is a scream where you wish to stop living for that moment, so you do not have to experience the emotional trauma unfolding before you. It is a sense of loss, but you do not know what you lost and how you will get it back again. You feel like you are dying, but know you have to keep living. You want to cry, but your burdens will not allow it. Your emotional pain shapes you into who you are and who you will become. This all seems negative, yet I promise you can turn it into something that can benefit you.

There is one big difference between physical and emotional pain: Nobody can see the emotional pain you are going through. It is not an outward battle where everyone can witness your strength. No, it is a battle you must fight in the darkest corners of your mind. It is a war you must fight every day. The truth is that we are all going through emotional pain that no one else knows about. We all have our secret struggles that no one else can see.

Knowing that everybody is going through the same thing is necessary for understanding something fundamental to life: Everyone is shaped by the pain they have been through. Nobody is that different from you. Sometimes, it feels like there are divides everywhere you look. But if you remember that everyone goes through similar emotional pain, the rifts between people can slowly be broken down.

Emotional pain can teach another important lesson. I have found that something truly unique happens after you go through an emotional hell. When you come to the other side of the tunnel, and you will, the world looks a whole lot different. You start to notice things you never did and appreciate what you took for granted. Going through unimaginable pain has a way of opening your eyes and helping you see things for what they are. You start to realize how beautiful everything is.

Only when you experience pain that hits you in your core can you understand that there is a light after all your hardship. You can never see the true elegance of life until it is ripped from you for a short time. Emotional pain can be a living hell, but it can also be one of the best things to happen to you. Because when it is all said and done, this agony leaves you much stronger and opens your eyes to how wonderful life truly is. With each new emotional scar, I promise you will learn never to take things for granted again. Pain of any kind reminds me that my days are numbered, and with that thought in mind, I enjoy each day even more.

Instead of pain, let me use another word: experience. At its core, that is what pain means—gaining experience. Every time you go through something painful, it helps build you into who you are. It creates your character and makes you strong. Pain of any kind sucks, but it also molds you into someone you can be truly proud of, as it did for me. With pain comes new experiences and new chances to see how strong you are. Look at both types of pain not as an inconvenience but as a chance to shake your world in a big way.

19 INSPIRATION

I am in fifth grade. It is that time of year again, time for another overnight.

My fourth-grade trip left a bad taste in my mouth. I became exhausted and could not keep myself together. I cried in front of my whole class, and my parents had to come to pick me up; I was embarrassed and mortified by how I acted. Needless to say, I had many feelings as I prepared for the fifth-grade trip.

To begin with, I was not even sure I wanted to go. The last year felt like a failure on my part, and I was not convinced I could face another one. My confidence was shaken, and I did not know how to get it back. This was one of the first times I felt unsure about myself.

Leading up to the trip, I kept going back and forth. At that point in my life, it was one of the most significant decisions I'd ever had to make. I did not know what to do; I was losing sleep over it. In retrospect, the stakes of this decision were small, but at the time, it meant realizing that I would always have to make hard choices like this. By the very nature of my disability, I would be put into situations where I would have to decide whether it was a good idea to participate in activities. I was starting to understand that my health would always impact decisions for my future.

Deciding whether to go on this overnight felt like standing on the precipice of all other future choices. All this coming at me when I was just eleven years old felt monumental. With all these thoughts storming, I was always on edge. I talked with my parents, my psychologist, and the school counselor. One thing became apparent: They would only be able to help me so much, and when it came down to it, I would need to make the final decision.

One day, my mother took me to a doctor's appointment. Afterward, she asked if I wanted to stop for a drink on the way home, and I speedily agreed. We gave the employee our order at the drive-through window, and as we waited for the drinks, he could see that I was in a bad mood. He asked me if everything was okay. I responded that I just had a lot on my mind. He looked me straight in the eye, and I will never forget his words.

He said, "I understand. I have days like that, too. But you know what I do when I have those bad days? I think it is all about my attitude. If I tell myself I will have a good attitude, I know I will have a good day. You need to change your perspective. Just be happy; it is all about your attitude. If you have a good attitude, then you will have a good day."

I thanked him for those kind words, then we got our drinks and left. On the way home, I turned his words over in my mind. Obviously, they did not help me with my current decision, but they did help me with something else. In times of struggle, I always look for words or ideas to give me some inspiration. The employee's words were undoubtedly that, but I did not expect it to come from a random stranger.

This event helped me in two ways. The first was that, with his words, I was able to choose to have a good attitude, and the decision for the overnight became clear. I would not go on this one, but would strengthen myself for the next one. I was surprised that by changing my outlook, I could make the right choice.

The second thing I realized was that inspiration can come from any place you look. I never thought the words I needed to hear would come out of a drive-through window, but incredibly, they did. It made me realize that motivation is all around me and can sometimes come at unexpected times. One day, you could be walking down the street, and boom, a little nugget of inspiration comes out of nowhere, gift-wrapped just for you. This idea keeps giving me hope for a better tomorrow.

I like to think that life is meant to inspire. You can become inspired daily and make the world a better place once you understand what a gift inspiration is. You will change not only your life, but also the world around you. However, before beginning to wield this incredible power, I would like to explain the big difference between inspiration and being inspired.

Inspiration is a moment of motivation, but being inspired is what you do with that motivation. Inspiration happens all around you and can come at any time, but it will never amount to anything unless you use it to motivate yourself to make the world better than it was when you found it. That is what it truly means to be inspired.

What is inspiration? What does it feel like when found? These are difficult questions to answer. When you find something that inspires you, you experience a feeling of excitement. It's like the whole world is brand new to you. You feel rejuvenated, and soon, you feel like you can take on the entire world by yourself. You hold on to this excitement, which can help you see a better version of yourself.

But that is not all—this feeling also leads you to the necessary steps to achieve any goal you set. If you can hold on to this inspiration and use it as motivation, there is so much you can do with it. You can make the world much brighter than you ever thought it could be. When truly inspired, you can turn dreams into reality, discover yourself, and live one of the best parts of the human experience. Inspiration is so powerful; it can open your eyes to what it truly means to be human. It can reveal the significance you can have in the world.

Simply put, being inspired provides the knowledge that no matter who you think you are, you can make this world better than it was before you got here. No matter what you feel, know that you are essential. That is what inspiration means. You have the opportunity to change the world in a big way. You matter.

Inspiration can come from anything. The magical thing is that it does not have time or reason. It happens whether you are ready or not. It can come from a book, a song, or even a quote. Even a random person off the street, like it did for me. The fact that inspiration can be found all over proves that the world wants to be explored. It is your job to find inspiration and turn it into motivation. Inspiration demands that it be found, so always look for it.

Motivation is entirely subjective. It can be found all around, but you must discover what inspires and motivates *you*. It is different for every person. Once you learn what motivates you, you will find a whole new world of possibilities out there.

Where you find that inspiration all comes down to you. If you are willing to look for it, you will find inspiration everywhere, although you must sift through it until you find what inspires you specifically. If you understand these ideas and can implement them, you will find the necessary inspiration to do great things. Once you can find what inspires you, there is no telling how far you can go and what you can accomplish.

When you look around at the world you are in, it is easy to think the world is how it is and will stay that way. Some people tell you that you should not make waves and that you must live in the confines of the world as it is. This leaves little room for inspiration. Yet, the world is this way because of others who were inspired to improve their lives. You can do the same; you cannot let the naysayers get to you. There is inspiration everywhere you look. You can use it to make your life more extraordinary than it was before. Never believe that you must accept your reality; if you keep pushing yourself, the world will improve, and so will your reality.

Inspiration comes to those who decide to take on a more significant role and change the world. Be someone who is not content to let life pass you by without moving more than just the dirt it takes to bury you. Within you is incredible potential to bring the world into a new and better era. It is inspiration that gives you a key to unlock your full potential. However, you must look around for that inspiration and use it to motivate you to new heights.

When you wake up each morning, there is no telling what the day will hold. Yet, if you start each day looking for inspiration, each new day will seem like a unique chance to help the world. Not only that, but inspiration also has a funny way of being contagious. You never know who you will inspire in turn, and they have yet to learn who they will inspire. You can be the inspiration someone needs not to give up and keep on fighting.

Let me leave you with a challenge: Always look for your inspiration wherever it may be, and try to live your life in a way that inspires others. If you can live with these two ideals, you will find greater joy and fulfillment. Inspiration is a moment of motivation, but being inspired is what you do with that motivation. Inspiration happens all around you and can come at any time, but it will never amount to anything unless you use it to motivate yourself to make the world better than it was when you found it. That is what it truly means to be inspired.

Let me put it another way. Life is meant to move you, and in turn, you are supposed to move the world.

20 THE CHAMPION IS NAMED

It was as if everything was moving in slow motion. The only thing I could hear was the sound of my heartbeats, which I knew were numbered. It seemed to drag on forever as the knife moved closer to its target. I closed my eyes, ready for everything to stop and nothing to begin.

When the blade was half an inch from puncturing my stomach, I stopped and stared at it. I had one final decision to make. I could end everything, stop the regret, the tears, the anger, the voices of doubt; in one motion, I could give up and make the pain stop. Let me tell you, that was so damn tempting. To end it all, I wanted to move that last half an inch and finish everything.

I looked down; I could not bring myself to finish the job. Why could I not do it? I was looking at the knife and knew for damn sure that I wanted it to be over. Suddenly, I heard a voice from my past. I heard my younger self saying, "I can do it by myself."

When I was younger, I was determined to do things by myself. Even when I was a small child, I was looking for independence, and at that age, that meant completing tasks on my own. Whenever someone, be it a friend or a family member, would try to help me with something, I would always look at them and say, "I can do it by myself." It became my mantra, but only in the later years of high school did I understand what I meant when I said it.

After many complex challenges, I understood that when I recited my mantra, I was saying that nothing was ever out of my reach and that I could accomplish anything I put my mind to. Saying "I can do it by myself" meant that whatever came my way, I would meet it head-on and never back down, come hell or high water. Even as a young kid, I never wanted my CP to define what I could and could not do; there was never a challenge too big for me to overcome if I believed in who I was and what I wanted out of life. "I can do it by myself" was a battle cry to gather my strength and courage for whatever obstacle came my way.

I had not thought about my mantra in a long time, but it all returned to me in one second. Looking down at the knife, I said aloud, "I can do it myself." I said it to myself repeatedly. "I can do it myself. I can do it myself. I can do it myself." Each time I said it, I could feel my courage and strength returning and my voice getting stronger. As I continued to repeat it, the fire inside me was relit. In one second, it was like a movie played in my mind of all my greatest hits.

I saw all the surgeries I underwent and how strong I became because of them; I saw the countless hours of therapy I endured and how much I had improved myself, I saw the faces of my family and friends, who were always there to encourage me when I needed them. I saw the impact I had made on everyone around me and the impact they had made on me. I saw every obstacle I had ever overcome.

Suddenly, I felt tears stinging my eyes. They were no longer tears of pain, but of pride. I had been through so much and always fought until I won. Countless times I had been knocked back on my ass, but every single damn time, without fail, I would get up and fight back with newfound strength. Every single damn time I thought I was finished; I would always get back up off the ground and keep pushing forward. I had never been defeated before, and there was no way in hell I would be defeated now. No way in hell.

At that moment, I saw all I had been through and how much I had gained and achieved because of all my experiences. I knew I did not give up at any time in the past, and damn it, there was no way in hell I would give up now. I knew I had made my choice in my heart, and there was only one thing I could do. I could fight with everything I had left. I was battered and bruised, but knew I could not lose this battle. I did not know how or if I would win, but I knew I had to get back in the ring because I was about to fight for my life. In that one second, I fought tooth and nail against my demons, never giving an inch, never backing down. I got back up every time I was knocked down and kept fighting. I kept battling till I had nothing left, and even then, I kept pushing myself more and more.

My demons were strong, but I needed to be stronger. With strength born from trials and tribulations and pain and gain, I started to fight off my enemy. With power I did not even know I still had, I fought like I had nothing to lose. I was beyond tired, but I was now a man on a mission. One way or another, this was going to end right here right now. Live or die, I was proud of who I was and that was never going to be taken away from me. Proud of every scar I had, proud of every time I was brought to the brink of quitting but did not, and proud of the man I had become.

I was battling with everything I had left. Awakened in me was a power I did not even know I had. It took all my strength, but I moved the knifepoint from my stomach to the top of my hand. The smoke cleared, the battle was decided. I was left breathing, and my trophy was a new scar: a cut on the top of my hand.

Seeing the blood oozing from the wound I'd inflicted was just the jolt I needed. The sight woke me from the daze I had been in. It was like my system had rebooted, and I had emerged from a deep sleep. I was myself again. I knew I needed help; I called my sister in the morning and told her what I had done. She told me I also needed to tell my parents.

I called and told them I had cut myself on the top of my hand and needed help. Together, we decided that I needed to see the college's psychologist. I went to the psychologist's office and started telling my story. I ended up talking with two different psychologists. In a phone discussion with them and my parents, it was decided that I would come home and get the help I needed. Just the idea of coming home lifted a considerable weight off my shoulders. However, at the same time, I felt like I was a loser. I felt like a failure, and nothing would make me feel any different, or so I thought.

My father told me he was flying out to New York to pick me up. But he was not coming in until later that night. After I left the psychologist's office, I felt famished; it was the first time I had felt hungry in the last two days. I went to the cafeteria and got food, a lot of food. I do not remember what I ate, but I had never tasted food so delicious.

I guess my parents had told family members that I was leaving school. Throughout the day, I got calls from my family telling me it was okay to go home. They talked to me about their own struggles, and after hearing their stories, I felt so much better. Knowing I was not alone was reassuring.

My father came to get me, and we packed up the dorm room. I wanted to get the hell out of dodge and leave New York. I was now looking to my future. I knew I needed help and would get it when I got home. I was also excited. Having hit rock bottom, I now had a new chance. I stepped on the plane with a mission in mind. I wanted to rebuild myself, not just who I was before New York. No, I was ready to rebuild myself stronger and better than ever.

It took me a couple of years after leaving New York to see everything clearly. What I had done that night, cutting myself, was not the act of a desperate man. No, it was the catalyst I needed. I now understand that I did not pick up that knife out of anger and sadness. I held that knife with every experience I had been through. Hurting myself was the awakening I needed to love myself for who I am. Learn from my mistakes, don't wait around for life, live it now. I got very good at dealing with life's many challenges, but in doing so, I forgot that I am more than just my struggles. I only learned to love myself when it was almost too late. For so long I was filled with self-loathing. It grew so strong that I thought the only way out was suicide. I was wrong, so very wrong. don't hate yourself, it just not worth it.

    Take it from someone with a lot of regrets like me, don't waste a damn second; it can all be gone in a blink of an eye. Everything I have talked about in this book really comes down to that. Find a way to love yourself. At the end of the day, that is what matters. It took me almost committing suicide to love myself. Don't wait too long and end up like I did. Love yourself now, today and always. You're worth more than you can ever imagine.

21 BECAUSE YOU WERE HERE

Now you know my story. The good and the bad. Honestly, there are some parts I am not so proud of, and there are some instances I would never change. However, there is more happiness than pain in my past.

Past—that is a funny word. I just told you my past, but at the same time, I want to let it go. I think at the end of the day that's what we all need to try. Letting go of the past, but never forgetting its lessons. I tried to kill myself. I was ready to end it all, but I chose not to. Call it what you will, but I got a second chance at life, and I know for damn sure I will not screw it up. I want to live and be proud of who I am. I want the world to be better because I was around.

Life ends; it is a sad fact. One moment, you are here, and the next, you are not. You are on this earth for such a short time. Knowing your days are numbered, does that change how you should live? I hope your answer is yes. The ultimate goal of life is to make the world that much more beautiful than it was before you got here. To leave something here that will stand the test of time. Many years from now, when you are long gone, you want the world to be far superior because you were around. The measure of your life should be whether you moved more than just the dirt it takes to bury you. You should always strive to make each day better than the one that came before. When it is all said and done, the question you want to ask yourself is this: Did you live a life worth living, and was it one you were proud of?

In theory, this is a great goal, but how do you execute this plan? How do you live a life to be genuinely proud of? How do you leave a lasting impact? Is it enough just to be a good person, or do you need to push yourself to the next level and keep doing that your entire life? That is the question you should struggle with. Because it means that every day, when you wake up, you still are doing your best to grow yourself. Let me tell you from experience that the second you stop asking yourself those questions will be the day you start down a dark path that is hard to come back from. When your life comes to an end, and you look back, how can you know that what you did mattered and made any difference in the world? What did your life amount to? Was it one you could be proud of?

Because of everything I have been through, I feel confident in saying that I know how to live a fulfilling life. Wake up daily with a smile, and when your feet touch the floor, always set out to make the day count for something. Make someone smile, better yourself, laugh as much as possible, and be a positive light for the people around you. I promise you will lead a life worth living if you can do this.

Look, I don't know shit about many things. But if there is one thing I think I know well, it is how to play the hand of life that has been dealt to me. Life is not always going to be fair. However, if you decide to live a life to the fullest, it will not matter that life does not always play by the rules. With all the crap that can happen to you, there is one thing you must always remember: If you want to leave an impact on this world, make damn sure you are always growing.

You have the power to change the world if you want to. Inside of you is the potential to shake the world in a big way; never forget that. Life gives you an expiration date; you never know when it will be. Live your life to the fullest, and never take anything for granted, because it goes by fast, like the snap of your fingers. But that is what makes it even more special. Be happy, fight for things you believe in, drink in your time with your loved ones, always bet on yourself, and hold on to hope no matter what.

So, with all that in mind, I have a final challenge for you. Wake up each day and live a life worth living, one you are proud of, and you make damn sure you leave this world that much more beautiful because you were here.

ACKNOWLEDGEMENTS

Special <u>recognition</u> goes to my publishers at Journey Institute and editor Jessica Medberry, for taking a chance on someone like me. For helping me see my dream turn into a reality. Thank you.

ABOUT THE AUTHOR

David Last is from Denver Colorado and went to high School at Denver Jewish Day School. He was diagnosed with Cerebral Palsy, (C.P.) when he was twelve months old. An avid reader who enjoys playing video games *Forged by Limitations* is his first book. In it he recounts the struggles and triumphs of living with C.P. His hope is that by sharing his story he can inspire others.

JOURNEY INSTITUTE PRESS

Journey Institute Press is a non-profit publishing house created by authors to flip the publishing model for new authors. Created with intention and purpose to provide the highest quality publishing resources available to authors whose stories might otherwise not be told.

JI Press focusses on women, BIPOC, and LGBTQ+ authors without regard to the genre of their work.

As a Publishing House, our goal is to create a supportive, nurturing, and encouraging environment that puts the author above the publisher in the publishing model.

Storytellers Publishing is an Imprint of Journey Institute Press, a division of 50 in 52 Journey, Inc.

NOTE: The world of publishing has changed dramatically. This has also affected authors and their ability to let readers know about their books. Today, most people buy books based on word of mouth.

If you would like to help this author, please consider leaving an honest review of this book on retail sites and book community sites.

www.ingramcontent.com/pod-product-compliance
Lightning Source LLC
Chambersburg PA
CBHW030241010526
44107CB00030B/1296/J